Conducting the Web De
IT Manager Guide with Interview Questions

Janet Burleson

RAMPANT TECHPRESS

I dedicate this book to my husband Don, my one true love and best friend.

--- Janet Burleson

Conducting the Web Designer Job Interview
IT Manager Guide with Interview Questions

By Janet Burleson

Copyright © 2004 by Rampant TechPress. All rights reserved.

Printed in the United States of America.

Published by: Rampant TechPress, Kittrell, North Carolina, USA

IT Job Interview Series: Book # 7

Series Editor: Don Burleson

Editors: John Lavender, Janet Burleson and Cliff Muncy

Production Editor: Teri Wade

Production Manager: Linda Webb

Cover Design: Bryan Hoff

Illustrations: Mike Reed

Printing History: September 2004 for First Edition

The information provided by the authors of this work is believed to be accurate and reliable, but because of the possibility of human error by our authors and staff, Rampant TechPress cannot guarantee the accuracy or completeness of any information included in this work and is not responsible for any errors, omissions, or inaccurate results obtained from the use of information or scripts in this work. Many of the designations used by computer vendors to distinguish their products are claimed as Trademarks. All names known to Rampant TechPress to be trademark names appear in this text as initial caps.

Flame Warriors illustrations are copyright © by Mike Reed Illustrations Inc.

Special thanks to Cliff Muncy, Jeff Hunter, Adam Haeder, Mike Ault, Shannon Lesane and Don Burleson for their contributions to this publication.

ISBN: 0-9745993-0-1

Library of Congress Control Number 2004101896

Table of Contents

Using the Online Code Depot 1
Conventions Used in this Book 2
Acknowledgements 4
Preface 5
   IMPORTANT NOTE: 6

Chapter 1 - Web Designer Evaluation 9

Introduction 9
Preparing the Web Designer Job Offering 10
   Preparing the Incentive Package 10
   Defining the Required Job Skills 13
   Basic IT Skills 15
Characteristics of the Professional Web Designer 16
Sample Job Sheet for a Senior Web Designer 18
Conclusion 21

Chapter 2 - Successful Web Designer Qualities .. 22

Résumé 22
Evaluating Employment History 23
   Fraudulent Work History 23
Evaluating Personal Integrity 24
Evaluating Academic History 25
   The Quality of Education 25
   Rating College Education 27
   College Major and Job Suitability 27
   International Degrees 29
   Advanced Degrees and Programming Professionals 30
   The New Graduate 30
Personality of the Professional Web Designer 32
   Self-confidence 33
   A Curious Nature 34
   A Tenacious Disposition 35
   Polite Manners 35
   Self-Motivating 36

Attention to Detail *38*
Conclusion 39

Chapter 3 - Roles for the Web Designer 41
Finding a well-rounded candidate 41
Web Designer Job Roles 42
Application Tuning *44*
Troubleshooting *44*
Communication Skills *45*
Conclusion 46

Chapter 4 - Initial Screening 48
Preparation 48
The High Cost of Attrition and Hiring Overhead 50
Choosing Viable Candidates 50
Dealing with IT Headhunters 52
General Evaluation Criteria 53
Gleaning Demographics from the Candidate 56
The Selection Process 59
Résumé Evaluation 59
Résumé Red Flags *60*
Evaluating a Web Designer's Training *62*
Telephone Screening 64
Technical Pre-Testing 66
Developing Questions for Interviews 67
The IT Candidate's Demeanor *68*
Appropriate Appearance *70*
Conducting the Background Check 72
Conclusion 73

Chapter 5 - Preparing for the On-site Interview .. 75
Choosing the Right Questions 75
Questions from the Candidate 76
Telephone Pre-interview Questions 77
Conclusion 78

Chapter 6 - On-Site Interview Questions 79
Most Commonly Asked 79

Chapter 7 - What Candidates Always Ask 86
Two-way Street 86

Chapter 8 - What a Candidate Should Never Ask 88
Best of the Worst 88
Just for fun 90

Chapter 9 - The Job Offer 91
Negotiations 91
After the Job Offer 92
Evaluating you! 93
Getting Along on the Job 94
Complaints from the Scientist Web Designer 94
Complaints from the Gung-Ho Web Designer 95
Complaints from the Empathetic Web Designer 95
Conclusion 96

Chapter 10 - The Technical Interview 97
IMPORTANT NOTE: 97
Basic Web Designer Questions 97
Adobe Photoshop Questions 107
FTP Questions 117
JavaScript Questions 121
PHP Scripting Questions 129
Dreamweaver Questions 137
MySQL Questions 147
SQL Questions 152
MS FrontPage Questions 156
Flash MX 2004 Questions 164
Perl Script Questions 169
Apache Questions 175
Security Questions 178
Java and J2EE Versions 188

Table of Contents

Qualifications	*188*
Java Interview Questions	190
J2EE Telephone Pre-interview Questions	198
J2EE Development Concepts	204
Java Server Pages (JSP)	*216*
Java Beans	*226*
C Programming Questions	233
C ++ Questions	244
Non-Technical Questions	254
Policies, Processes and Procedures	*272*
Quality	*274*
Commitment to Task	*276*
Planning, Prioritizing and Goal Setting	*278*
Attention to Detail	*280*
Initiative	*283*

Index ... 285
About Janet Burleson ... 289
About Mike Reed ... 290

Using the Online Code Depot

Your purchase of this book provides you with complete access to the online code depot that contains the sample questions and answers.

All of the interview questions in this book are located at the following URL:

www.rampant.cc/job_web_design.htm

All of the sample tests and questions in this book will be available for download, ready to use for your next interview.

If you need technical assistance in downloading or accessing the scripts, please contact Rampant TechPress at info@rampant.cc

Get the Advanced Oracle Monitoring and Tuning Script Collection

The complete collection from Mike Ault, the world's best DBA.

Packed with 590 ready-to-use Oracle scripts, this is the definitive collection for every Oracle professional DBA.

It would take many years to develop these scripts from scratch, making this download the best value in the Oracle industry.

It's only $39.95 (less than 7 cents per script!)

To buy for immediate download, go to
http://www.oracle-script.com/

Conventions Used in this Book

It is critical for any technical publication to follow rigorous standards and employ consistent punctuation conventions to make the text easy to read.

However, this is not an easy task. Within computer programming technologies there are many varieties of notations that can confuse a reader. Some programming syntax, such as J2SE and J2SE SDK, use CAPITAL letters, while programming parameters and procedures have varying naming conventions in the documentation.

It is also important to remember that many commands are case sensitive, and will be left in their original executable form, and never altered with italics or capitalization. Hence, all Rampant TechPress books follow these conventions:

Source Code – Anything that might appear in a program, including code snippets, keywords, method names, variables names, class names, and interface names will use a `monospaced font`.

New Terms – An *Italics font* will be used for all new terms, book titles and for emphasis.

Parameters and Placeholders – A *lowercase italics font* will be used to identify any command-line parameters or placeholders required by the user.

Commands and Programmer Programs – A `**bold monospaced font**` will be used to identify binaries or command-line applications that will need to be typed by the user.

Products – All products that are known to the author are capitalized according to the vendor specifications (IBM, DBXray, Sun Microsystems, etc). All names known by Rampant TechPress to be trademark names appear in this text as initial caps. References to UNIX are always made in uppercase.

Acknowledgements

This type of highly technical reference book requires the dedicated efforts of many people. As the author my work ends when I deliver the content. After each chapter is delivered, experienced copy editors polish the grammar and syntax. The finished work is then reviewed as page proofs and turned over to the production manager, who arranges the creation of the online code depot and manages the cover art, printing, distribution, and warehousing. In short, the author plays a small role in the development of this book, and I need to thank and acknowledge everyone who helped bring this book to fruition:

John Lavender, for his expert operational management skills.

Teri Wade, for her hard work formatting the manuscript and producing the page proofs.

Linda Webb, for the production management, including the coordination of the cover art, page proofing, printing, and distribution.

Jeff Hunter, for providing much of the front-matter and questions.

Adam Haeder, for contributing the Security questions.

Don Burleson, the love of my life, for giving me the inspiration and assistance that I needed to complete this project.

Shannon Lesane, for her contribution to the Web Design questions.

Cliff Muncy, for his contribution to the Web Design questions.

With my sincere gratitude,

Janet Burleson

Preface

After interviewing countless candidates for Web Designer-related positions, I am aware that it is getting harder to locate and retain qualified Web Designers. You must cull the best fit from hundreds of résumés. Success depends upon knowing exactly which skills you need and verifying that each candidate possesses acceptable levels of those skills.

That's where this book can be helpful. For both the new IT manager and the seasoned VP, the various levels within the Web Designer position will be explained to illustrate screening and interview techniques.

Some common misconceptions about the Web Designer position will be clarified and tips will be provided on how to successfully interview a candidate for this type of position.

Few IT managers, especially in smaller companies, have extensive formal training in interviewing and hiring techniques. In most instances the interviewers' primary full-time responsibilities lie elsewhere.

In many cases IT managers do not have a clear idea of the skills and personal characteristics the job candidate should possess, or an effective process for screening potential employees. Yet nothing is more crucial to the success of the organization than doing everything possible to ensure that the selected candidate is the best fit for the available position.

This book will provide effective techniques for finding committed employees who are able to function at a high level on the job. By eliminating guesswork and rejecting the random hit-or-miss approach that is based on the instincts of the interviewer and little else, the employer can hire confidently.

To help find, hire, and retain suitable Web Designers, background evaluation tips will be provided for identifying the best candidates.

For the technical interview, sample questions and answers are also provided. A non-technical evaluation section is provided to help determine whether the candidate's personality is a good match for the organization and whether the candidate will be able to integrate seamlessly with your shop's particular culture.

Of course, there is no magic formula for determining if a candidate can perform properly, and no single screening test to ensure that you will properly evaluate a candidate's ability. However, if the employer and candidate are properly prepared, then filling the position successfully becomes less of a risk.

It is my hope that this book will become an indispensable tool for identifying, interviewing, and hiring top-notch Web Designers.

IMPORTANT NOTE:

It is not the intention of this work to provide a comprehensive technical exam, and the technical questions in this book and the code depot are only intended to be examples of questions that could be used to select the appropriate candidate. The only way to accurately evaluate the technical skills of a job applicant is to employ the services of an experienced technical person to conduct an in-depth technical interview and skills assessment.

Also note that the expected answers for the questions are highly dependent upon the version of the product and the candidate's interpretation of the question.

Every attempt has been made to format the questions as version neutral as possible, but each new release of every product brings hundreds of changes and new features, and these example questions may not be appropriate for your version.

For optimal results, it is best to have an experienced technical person administer the technical interview questions presented in this book.

Web Designer Evaluation

CHAPTER 1

Introduction

One of the results of the surge in the Internet's popularity is an ever-increasing demand for top-notch Web Designers and Web technology developers. As more companies continue to utilize a Web presence for business purposes, the demand for skilled Web Designers increases. However, this mushrooming need for Web Designers has created a vastly disparate job pool. Job skills range from software engineers with PhDs in Information Systems acquired from top U.S. universities with 20 years' experience, to semi-qualified Web Designer trainees with 90 days' or less experience.

The result of the explosive growth of the Web technology industry is the evolution of a two-tiered job market. Many top-rated universities teach Web programming as part of their undergraduate Computer Science or Information Technology curriculum and produce Web Designers for career tracks in large corporations.

At the same time, trade schools and community colleges educate hundreds of thousands of capable Web Designers and developers. No matter what the economic climate, large corporations historically actively recruit their entry-level talent for mission-critical systems development from prestigious university programs.

Written with the IT manager in mind, this book provides useful insight into the techniques commonly used to identify the characteristics that make a successful Web Designer job candidate.

Preparing the Web Designer Job Offering

One point that bears repeating is that top-notch experienced Web Designers are hard to find and tend to be well compensated, while inexperienced Web Designers are easy to find and hire.

On the high end, Web Designers with over 10 years' IT programming experience and graduate degrees typically command salaries ranging from $70,000 to $101,000 per year, depending on geographical location and individual skill.

The first step in hiring a Web Designer is determining the skill set and level of skill required, and preparing an incentive package. If the IT environment is mission-critical, then a seasoned Web Designer with at least 5 years of experience is the safest choice. Candidates, however, with high skill levels and many years of experience often require incentives to abandon their present employment.

Preparing the Incentive Package

If a top-notch senior programming professional is desired, it might be surprising to find them in short supply, even in a down job market. While every manager knows that salary alone cannot guarantee employee loyalty, there are a host of techniques used by IT management to attract and retain top-notch Web Designers.

Web Designers like to use the latest hardware and software!

In addition to a competitive salary, some of the techniques used to entice potential Web Designers include:

Flex time - Burnout can be a real problem among Web Designers who must typically work evenings, weekends, and holidays to stay current with many demanding and sometimes conflicting project tasks. Many companies offer formal comp-time policies or institute a four-day workweek, allowing the Web Designer to work four, 10-hour days per week.

Telecommuting - Many Web Designers are allowed to work at home only visiting the office once per week for important face-to-face meetings.

Golden handcuffs - Because a high base salary does not always reduce attrition, many IT managers use yearly bonuses to retain employees. Golden handcuffs may take the form of a Management by Objective (MBO) structure, whereby the Web Designer receives a substantial annual bonus for meeting management expectations. Some companies implement golden handcuffs by paying the employee a huge signing bonus (often up to $50,000) and requiring the employee to return the bonus if he or she leaves the company in less than three years. However, don't be surprised to find that some competing companies will reimburse the Web Designer to repay a retention bonus.

Fancy job titles - Because Web Designers command high salaries, many are given honorary job titles other than simply Web Designer. These include Web Business Analyst, Web Designer Analyst, Web Technology Developer, and Web Systems Engineer. Other Web Designer titles may include Vice President of Web Engineering, Chief Technologist, and the new job title (used by Bill Gates), Chief Software Architect.

Specialized training - Companies commonly reward Web Designers by sending them to conferences and training classes and an entire industry is built around these large educational events. For example, every year thousands of Web Designers gather for one week in San Francisco for the JavaOne[SM] conference. Here, great minds in programming get together to network, learn and celebrate technology, innovation, community, and education.

Defining the Required Job Skills

A number of Web Designers mistakenly believe that the job of the Web Designer is purely technical. In reality, the Web Designer must be creative, efficient and knowledgeable with graphic design principles. They should also be skilled with image creation, manipulation and placement. Because Web Designers are heavily involved in all phases of the Web presence development lifecycle, they must have excellent interpersonal and communication abilities as well as technical skills.

Remember, knowledge of simple web page design is often not enough. An understanding of operating systems and computer-science theory is beneficial as well. That is why many employers like to hire Web Designers who also have a background in computer science, information systems, or business administration.

Code Depot Username = reader, Password = nova

It's also critical to remember that a technical skill certification only tells employers that the job candidate successfully passed a certification test on the technical aspects of a particular technology. In the real world, a technical certification is just one of many criteria used to evaluate a Web Designer job candidate. Other criteria include the following:

Excellent Communication Skills - As one of the key stakeholders in any new Web presence development project, the Web Designer must possess exceptional communication skills. Effective communication skills not only include speaking but strong proficiencies in reading and writing as well.

In many Web technology development shops, it is the responsibility of the Web Designer or developer to communicate technical and sometimes highly complex

Preparing the Web Designer Job Offering

information to top-level management as well as other public groups. As the central technical guru, he or she must be able to explain concepts clearly in terms of the big picture. The audience may consist of all stakeholders including management, users, DBAs, programmers and other Web Designers participating in strategic planning and architectural reviews.

Formal Education - Many employers require Web Designers to have a bachelor's degree in Computer Science or Information Systems. For advanced positions such as a Principle Software Architect or Enterprise Development Architect, many employers prefer a Master's degree in Computer Science or a Master's in Business Administration (MBA).

Real-World Experience - This requirement is the catch-22 for newbies who possess only a technical certification. A common complaint among those who have technical certifications but no job experience is that they cannot get experience without a job, and they cannot get a job without experience. This is especially true in a tight job market.

Problem Solving Abilities - A successful candidate should also have the ability to translate raw concepts from vague design specs and paper-based storyboards, through prototypes, and all the way to a finished product. When analyzing problems in development, experienced Web Designers are able to recommend and implement effective solutions throughout all phases of development. They possess a deep-seated desire to develop innovative learning and teaching products and show profound capabilities for learning new topics. With excellent problem solving and organizational skills, a good candidate will possess the ability to evaluate information while making efficient architectural and design decisions.

Knowledge of Object-Oriented Design Theory - In addition to mastering the technical details required for the certification exams, the successful Web Designer must have an understanding of object-oriented design methodologies. This includes intimate knowledge of object-oriented design theory, object-oriented application design, CRC methods, design patterns as well as object-oriented modeling with Unified Modeling Language (UML).

Basic IT Skills

Because the Web Designer is often called upon to participate in critical projects in the IT department, a broad background is often desirable. Much of this basic IT knowledge is taught in academic Computer Science and Information Technology programs. Non- Web Designer job skills include:

System Analysis & Design - Many Web Designers must take an active role in analyzing and designing new web based application systems. Hence, knowledge of relational databases, data flow diagrams, CASE tools, entity-relation modeling, and design techniques enhance the Web Designer's scope of ability.

Database Design - Depending on the application being designed, many Web Designer jobs require knowledge of some database theory, STAR schema design, and data modeling techniques.

Data Security Principles - An understanding of database security, including role-based security, is useful, especially for US Government positions.

XML and Web Services - Knowledge of XML and Web Services (UDDI, SOAP, ebXML, WDSL) is essential when designing distributed enterprise systems.

Change Control Management - In some cases, the Web Designer will be responsible for utilizing version control and code sharing systems to ensure that changes to the production code base are properly coordinated. Knowledge of third-party change control tools, such as the UNIX Source Code

Control System (SCCS), CVS, Oracle SCM, or Continuus is essential when Change Control Management is necessary.

Now that some of the required skills are understood, a review of the importance of technical certification is warranted. Certification can be used as one of several minimum employment requirements.

However, as interviewers frequently discover, certification provides no guarantee that a candidate has real Web Designer development expertise. It does however show that the candidate has enough knowledge to pass the certification test.

Characteristics of the Professional Web Designer

Many Web development shops have hundreds of technology workers. However, retention efforts are normally focused on seasoned Web Designers, whose knowledge of the company's application systems is not easily transferred to replacements.

In some Web development shops, the Web Designer may fill many roles. In addition to the traditional responsibilities found in software engineering, the Web Designer is often called upon to serve as a system architect, a database administrator, or a system administrator. He or she may also be asked to serve as an "informaticist" (a functional IT professional with an MS in computer science who is also trained in professional areas, such as medicine, business management, or accounting).

A first rate Web Designer might possess the following attributes:

Has earned at least one professional degree or certification - Having a degree such as MD, JD, MBA, MSEE, or CPA, in addition to an undergraduate degree, makes an employee a valuable asset, and one difficult to replace in the open job market.

Has graduated from a competitive university - Web Designers must be self-starting and highly motivated to be effective. These qualities are often shared by those who've gained entrance into competitive universities with rigorous admission standards. These schools include most Ivy League schools, especially MIT, and universities with stellar reputations in Information Systems such as Purdue, the University of Texas, the University of California at Los Angeles, the University of San Diego, and the University of California at Berkeley.

Is trained in a special skill - Web Designers with specialized, difficult-to-find training are often in high demand. Such Web Designers have skills in areas such as ERP Systems (Oracle 11i, SAP, BaaN), Relational Database Technologies (Oracle, MySQL, PostGress), and J2EE Platforms (Oracle9iAS, BEA WebLogic, IBM WebSphere).

Active in the Web Designer community - Many good Web Designers participate in local user groups, present techniques, and publish in many of the programming related periodicals such as Dr. Dobbs.

Is recognized as a Web Design expert - A sure sign of a top-notch Web Designer is someone who comes to the forefront of audiences by publishing a book, writing a magazine article, or appearing as a conference speaker.

Possesses irreplaceable knowledge of an institution's enterprise systems - If the employee serves in a mission-critical role such as Chief Architect or Principal Software Engineer, that employee's departure may create a vacuum in the Application Development Department.

Sample Job Sheet for a Senior Web Designer

Applicants for any Web Designer position are expected to meet all the requirements in mission-critical areas, including education, experience, certification, writing credits, personal characteristics, and legal standing. Here is a sample Web Designer job requirement sheet:

Sample Web Designer Job Sheet

These are the minimum job requirements for the position of Senior Web Designer Enterprise Developer. The HR department will pre-screen all candidates for the following job skills and experience.

Education

Persons should have a Bachelor's and a Master's Degree, preferably from a recognized technology institution. At a minimum, the candidate is expected to possess a four-year degree from a fully-accredited university in a discipline such as Computer Science, Software Engineering, or Engineering (electrical, mechanical, or chemical), or a BA or MBA in Information Systems (from an AACSB accredited university).

Work Experience

The candidate should have five or more years of programming experience in object-oriented programming, two or more years programming experience with the (insert language here), and three or more years experience programming in UNIX/Linux system environments.

Web Designer Certification

The Web Designer candidate must have earned a platform/language specific certification at some time in the last 10 years.

Publishing and Research

The candidate should show an active interest in publishing programming research by participating in user groups and publishing articles, books, and columns on the subject. These include:

Books. Submitting proposals for publication to Web Designer technical book publishers or any other recognized academic publication company.

Articles for academic journals. Publishing articles in academic journals such as the *Journal of the IEEE*, *Management Science*, *Journal of Management Information Systems* and the *Journal of Systems & Software*.

Conference papers. Writing papers and presenting at conferences such as Oracle World, JAOO, and Colorado Software Summit.

Articles in trade publications. Writing articles for a trade publications such as *Dr. Dobbs Journal*.

Personal Integrity

This position requires designing and coding mission-critical applications and accessing confidential data, so all candidates are required to sign a waiver to disclose personal information.

The candidate must have no history of acts of moral turpitude, drug use, dishonesty, lying, cheating, or theft.

Security Clearance

This position requires a Top Secret Security clearance. Therefore, candidates must provide proof of eligibility.

Additional Specialized Skills

The following specialized skills are desired:

- Bachelors or Masters Degree from a major university.
- Active US Secret, Top secret or Q-level security clearance.
- Working knowledge of Oracle9iAS Containers for J2EE (OC4J).
- Ability to use case design.
- Ability to work with human resource systems from Oracle11i, SAP, or PeopleSoft.
- Strong knowledge in UNIX scripting languages including KSH and BASH

Positions as a Web Designer have requirements that vary widely, and it is up to the IT manager to choose those qualities most suitable for the available position.

Conclusion

This chapter has been concerned with identifying the job requirements of a skilled and experienced Web Designer candidate and in preparing an incentive package. Next, the topic of how to evaluate the Web Designer for specific job skills will be covered.

CHAPTER 2

Successful Web Designer Qualities

Résumé

Determining the quality of a successful candidate starts with evaluating the résumé. This is a critical part of the selection process. In a tight job market, it is not uncommon for HR and IT management to receive hundreds of résumés. It is important that they understand how to fairly and efficiently pre-screen applicants and only forward qualified individuals to the hiring manager for an interview. Here are some techniques for assessing the job history of a Web Designer.

A good Web Designer will demonstrate persistence!

Evaluating Employment History

Without question, a critical appraisal of a Web Designer's work history is the single most important factor in résumé screening. In most cases, candidates without a significant amount of work history will need to spend an excessive amount of time learning their jobs, while a higher-paid, experienced, ready to perform candidate may be a better overall value for the hiring company.

Not all Web Design experience is equal. Many demanding Web application development shops provide exceptional training and experience, while others provide only glancing exposure to the Web Designer environment.

When evaluating the work experience of a Web Designer candidate, the following factors should be considered:

- **Job role** - Web Designer candidates who have held positions of responsibility in areas that require design and architecture decisions are often more qualified than those candidates for whom Web Designer skills were a part-time duty.

- **Employer-sponsored Web Designer education** - Within many large corporations, IT employees are encouraged and, in some cases, required to participate in annual training events to keep their skill sets current. One good indicator of how current an applicant's job skills are is how much on-the-job education is cited on his or her résumé. Employer-sponsored, yearly Web Designer training and participation in Web Designer groups and conferences are indications of a good background for a Web Designer.

Fraudulent Work History

In the soft market of the early twenty-first century, it is not uncommon for a desperate job candidate to forge a work history with a defunct dot-com. The guilty applicant hopes that this fraud will not be detected. This phenomenon presents the IT manager with a unique challenge in verifying employment history with a company that no longer exists or contacting job references who, perhaps, cannot even speak English.

In many cases, the HR staff tends to discount résumés with employment and educational history that cannot be completely verified. Many departments, frustrated with confirming overseas employment histories, never forward these types of résumés to the IT manager.

Evaluating Personal Integrity

It is always a good idea to perform a background check, which is easily obtained via various national services. Many companies require that a candidate not have any criminal convictions, except minor traffic violations. In some cases, a routine background check can reveal arrests and acts of moral turpitude.

A Web Designer's ongoing responsibilities often include designing and coding mission-critical applications with confidential data. Therefore, some companies require that all applicants for Web Designer or developer positions be expected to demonstrate the highest degree of personal and moral integrity.

In addition, background checks that reveal a history of drug use, dishonesty, lying, cheating, or theft may be grounds for immediate rejection. In some companies, all applicants are expected to sign a waiver to disclose personal information and are asked to submit to a polygraph exam.

Evaluating Academic History

While formal education is not always a predictor of success as a Web Designer, there can be no doubt that job candidates with advanced degrees from respected universities possess both the intelligence and persistence needed to be a top-notch Web Designer.

The Quality of Education

When evaluating the educational background of job candidates, it is important to remember that not all colleges are created equal. Many IT managers tend to select candidates from only the top tier colleges and universities because they rely on the universities to do the pre-screening for them.

For example, an IT professional who has been able to enroll in a top tier university clearly demonstrates high achievement, intelligence, and a very strong work ethic. At the other end of the spectrum, there are many IT candidates who have attended vocational schools, night schools, and non-accredited universities to receive bachelor's degrees in nontraditional study areas. In some cases, these IT professionals may lack the necessary technical and communicational skills required to succeed in the IT industry.

The type of degree a candidate has attained is also a factor in how suitable he or she is for the position. For example, an ABS or MS in Computer Science generally requires the IT job candidate to have a very strong theoretical background in mathematics and physics. Those with formal degrees in computer science tend to gravitate toward software engineering and software development fields that require in-depth knowledge about lower-level components in computer systems.

On the other hand, BS and MBA degrees in Information Systems offered by accredited business colleges (accredited by the American Assembly of Collegiate Business Schools, AACSB) tend to strike a balance between IT programming skills and business skills. The information systems degree candidate will have a background in systems analysis and design, as well as familiarity with functional program development for specific business processes.

Unlike computer science majors, information systems majors will have a background in accounting, finance, marketing, economics, and other areas of business administration that equip them to solve business problems.

Many IT shops save time by letting universities pre-screen Web Designer candidates. For example, MIT carefully screens grades and achievement, and this allows companies to choose computer science professionals from MIT with increased confidence in the candidate's possession of the required skills.

The type of job to be filled may determine the academic history required. For example, a basic Web Designer position may not require a four-year degree, while a lead Web Designer analyst for a large corporation may require a Master's degree from a respected university.

Note: This section is based on the author's experience in evaluating Web Designers and the HR policies of large Web application development shops. This section is in no way meant to discredit those Web Designer job applicants without the benefit of a college education as in many cases a self taught Web Designer may possess the skill and attributes necessary to successfully fill the Web Designer position.

Rating College Education

Many shops have an HR professional evaluate education, while other IT managers take it upon themselves to evaluate the technical quality of the Web Designer candidate's formal education. Fortunately, sources for rating colleges and universities can be found online. Many large corporations require that the job candidate's degree must be from a university possessing a first-tier or second-tier rating by *US News & World Report's* "America's Best Colleges" or degrees from exceptional universities (as listed in *The Gourman Report*).

Of course, not all jobs as a Web Designer require a college degree. For lower-level Web Designer positions, the formal academic requirements are less stringent, but the lead Web Designer developer for a large corporation must possess high intelligence, superb communications skills, and the drive and persistence that is most commonly associated with someone who has taken the time to invest in a quality education.

College Major and Job Suitability

There is a great deal of debate about what academic majors, if any, are the best indicators of future success as a Web Designer. However, it is well documented that different majors attract students with varying abilities. The following list describes some indicators used in large corporations for assessing the relative value of different college majors:

Engineers - Engineers tend to make great Web Designers, especially those with degrees in Electrical Engineering (EE). An engineering curriculum teaches logical thinking, algorithm design, and data structure theory that makes it easy for the engineer to quickly learn Web Design programming concepts. However, while engineers have unimpeachable technical skills, their oral and written communication skills are sometimes lacking. Therefore, IT managers should pay careful attention to communication skills when interviewing Web Designer applicants with engineering degrees.

Business Majors - Business majors make excellent Web Designers and analysts because of their training in finance, accounting, marketing, and other business processes. Many business schools also require matriculated students to take several courses in Information Technology. Of course, not all college business schools are equal. When evaluating a Web Design job seeker with a business major, screeners should ensure that the degree is from a business school accredited by the American Assembly of Collegiate Business Schools (AACSB). There are many tiers of business schools, offering vastly different levels of training.

Computer Science Majors - Computer scientists typically receive four years of extensive technical training, and are ideal candidates for the role of jobs requiring in-depth technical ability. However, like engineers, some computer scientists have less than desirable communications skills.

Music Majors - For many years, IBM recruited from the ranks of college musicians because hiring managers found that musicians possessed an ability in logical thinking that made them ideal candidates for IT skill training.

Math Majors - Math majors tend to possess excellent logical thinking skills and often possess a background in Computer Science. Like many quantitative majors, social and communications skills may be a concern.

Education Majors - Evaluation of education majors is extremely difficult because of the wide variation in quality between universities. Nationally, GRE test rankings by academic major show that education majors consistently rank in the lowest 25% of knowledge. Any applicant with an education major should be carefully screened for technical skills, and the college ranking checked in *US News & World Report's* "America's Best Colleges".

Some computer professionals are insecure about their vocabulary

International Degrees

A huge variation in quality exists among international degrees. Therefore, Web Designer candidates with international degrees should be carefully checked in *The Gourman Report of International Colleges and Universities*.

Some sub-standard overseas colleges have no entrance requirements and require little effort from the student. There has also been a rash of résumé falsifications of college degrees from overseas colleges. The fraudulent applicant is often relying on the

Evaluating Academic History

human resource department's inability to successfully contact the overseas school to verify the applicant's degree.

In sum, international degrees should be carefully scrutinized. It is recommended that, where appropriate, foreign language professionals are hired to write the letters to request verification of the graduate's attendance, and to obtain and translate the college transcript.

Advanced Degrees and Programming Professionals

The percentage of Web Designers for large corporations possessing an advanced degree (Master's or Doctorate) is increasing. While an advanced degree shows dedication to a professional position, the quality of the degree is of paramount concern.

A higher ranking should be given to an on-site Master's degree from a respected university than to a night school or "non-traditional" graduate school. These non-traditional schools often have far lower acceptance standards for students and are far less academically demanding than the top US graduate programs.

The New Graduate

Regardless of the educational experience of the graduate, there will likely be little in the applicant's background that will prepare him/her for the real-world business environment. Computer Science curricula tend to emphasize theoretical issues of interest to academicians that may have little direct bearing on the needs of the business.

The recent graduate may have grandiose visions of designing and maintaining whole Web enterprise systems. They may be very adept at writing code from scratch, but will rarely be called upon to do this.

Recent College graduates can be immature.

Instead, what is needed is someone who can work within the existing software system without crashing and burning the system. What's of major importance here is the ability to read OPC (Other People's Code). The candidate with the ability to slog through existing code and understand it is the candidate who will be able to add data and make changes to the company's Web presence without bringing operations to a grinding halt.

Moreover, the work that the new employee does on the Web Design will undoubtedly be modified and altered by others in the future, as new needs develop and hidden problem areas emerge. For this reason, a candidate who is able to show the technical interviewer that she has excellent documentation skills and habits can be much more of an asset to the company than someone who is not accustomed to submitting work that must be accessible to others. Several of the questions in Chapter 5 are useful in gauging these traits.

Personality of the Professional Web Designer

What is more important to managers, technical knowledge or personality? Many times, managers concentrate too much on technical skill, while overlooking a candidate's personality.

In almost every core job function mentioned previously, the Web Designer's work comprises interacting with vendors, users, DBAs, managers, and even other designers. With that in mind, the following professional personality traits are, or ought to be, embodied by the successful Web Designer.

Some Web Designers have split personalities.

These traits are important for people in almost any profession, but they are particularly important for the Web Designer. Let it be said of the successful candidate that he or she is creative, self-confident, curious, tenacious, polite, motivated, and a stickler for details.

For some Web Designers, everything is an emergency!

Self-confidence

Technology professionals that lack self-confidence, ask the manager's opinion on every decision no matter how large or small, and show no initiative, are not all-star material. This indecision may be acceptable for an entry-level Web Designer being supervised by a senior Web Designer, but the candidate should be expected to learn to depend on his or her own judgment for important decisions.

In interviews, questions must be asked about problems encountered and how the applicant would resolve the problems. Answers provided should reflect self-confidence.

A Curious Nature

Curiosity is a core trait of the Web Designer because the Web Design platform is constantly changing, and it is sometimes difficult to find examples and documentation for those changes in the short term. A Web Designer who is not curious is passive and reactive, while a curious Web Designer is proactive. The proactive Web Designer will install the latest version of the platform and find enhancements that will make their code more efficient and easier to read, and in many cases, will improve performance.

Beware of Web Designers who don't take initiative.

The curious Web Designer invests personal money to stay current. In interviews with potential candidates, questions should be asked about the books and professional publications the candidate relies upon. Needless to say, answers indicating sole reliance on "the documentation set" are not an indication of professional curiosity.

Because curiosity is a requirement for a good Web Designer, another set of interview questions should involve the various Web Design technologies and the constant flow of new versions and packages provided for the Web Designer. A top-flight Web Designer is not lacking in awareness of the Web Design technologies and tools.

A Tenacious Disposition

Like most disciplines in the IT industry, a Web Designer or developer requires bulldog-like tenacity for successful troubleshooting. The Web Designer should enjoy knuckling down on a problem and not giving up until an answer is found.

Many design problems can be solved if the Web Designer or developer tenaciously pursues solving them rather than giving up.

Polite Manners

A Web Designer works closely with other people. Therefore, tact is required when dealing with managers, users, DBAs, artists, photographers and even other developers.

Some Web Designers have a reputation for poor manners!

But here's a fact of life for developers or Web Designers: Project managers, DBAs, and users will bring forth unreasonable requests and impossible deadlines. The Web Designer must cultivate interpersonal skills to respond to such requests without burning bridges. Ill-will is fostered outside the application development department by a rude Web Designer or developer. The Web Designer must be polite, beginning in the job interview.

Self-Motivating

Employers recognize and value self-starting employees. These are employees who require little in the way of supervision and constant spoon-feeding. Much more in the way of self-motivation is expected from the Web Designer than other IT professionals; primarily because they are the ones that must take charge of critical architecture and design decisions to produce a successful system. In addition, successful Web Designers foresee and prevent problems early in the system design, and seasoned professionals know what factors can cause trouble if they are ignored.

Motivation is a major factor in successful job performance.

A self-motivated Web Designer will have a history of programming and debugging techniques that can be applied in making the most efficient use of his or her time during system development.

A self-aware Web Designer sees reality clearly.

In an interview, the successful Web Designer is able to respond to questions about Web Design language fundamentals, application development, and application deployment by talking about the systems they designed and coded. Therefore, the interviewer can craft questions about specific techniques to identify candidates who have actually been involved in a project's critical design and architectural issues.

Attention to Detail

Being detail-oriented is perhaps the most important trait for a Web Designer. Like most IT professionals, Web Designers are often described as having an "anal" personality for their attention to detail, after Sigmund Freud's theory of anal-retentive personalities.

Attention to detail is critical for quality Web Design.

A good Web Designer should not have to be told to crosscheck details or to document quirks observed during the design or coding phases. A detail-oriented or systematic person is early for an appointment and brings a PDA or calendar to an interview. Questions asked by the detail-oriented person should reflect the research conducted about the potential new employer.

Conclusion

This chapter has been concerned with the specific criteria for evaluating work and academic history. It also included an introduction to the most common personal characteristics of a top Web Designer. The next chapter will evaluate the roles of Web Designers and provide more insight into the characteristics of a successful Web Designer.

Fluency in Klingon may indicate a personality disorder.

Roles for the Web Designer

CHAPTER 3

Finding a well-rounded candidate

A good Web Designer candidate is able to articulate a solid knowledge of techniques in all areas of Web Design technologies, including coding and design, software configuration management, testing and debugging, use of the Web Designer technologies, 3rd party code reuse, and code documentation using standard documentation methods. In addition, a successful Web Designer in any organization must possess above-average communication skills.

Nit-picky Web Designers document everything!

Web Designer Job Roles

The job of a Web Designer means many things to many people. In many cases, the size of the employing company will determine what is required from a Web Designer. In a small shop, the duties are much broader than in corporations with teams of Web Designers and developers dedicated to specific projects.

The functions of the Web Designer can also be determined by other factors, such as whether or not the employer is doing custom development. Are they utilizing third-party packages that require integration? Will the application be Web-based and if so, will it be part of an application framework that is ASCII compliant? The interviewee and the interviewer must be prepared to discuss and understand what is expected of the Web Designer and his or her role within the company hierarchy.

When a project begins that involves Web technology development, be assured that shortly after the kickoff, many talents within the IT department will be involved, including computer programming, developing, and analysis. Web Designers will be involved from the start, interviewing end users, gathering business requirements, helping set expectations, and mulling over technical design issues. While design and coding remains the most crucial responsibility of the Web Designer, many application development shops include other functions as part of this job position. Here are some common job duties for both Web Designers and developers:

Produce Specifications - Work with end users and project managers to write specifications that meet client requirements for applications. The Web Designer/developer will then work with clients and other consultants to program and code applications according to those specifications.

Determine User Requirements - Gather and work with requirements. This often involves Use Cases, UML diagrams, ERD diagrams, and other prototypes. The candidate should understand that the Use Case document is probably the most important of the documenting requirements. It contains the "stories" of how the user will eventually be utilizing the system. It is important that the candidate demonstrate past success in working with customers in documenting Use Cases and ensuring that they are clearly understood throughout the project life cycle.

Test Application Functionality - Work with clients and other team members to test an application's functionality, performance, and load according to specifications. Is the candidate able to demonstrate success in automating tests, performing unit tests, or using a testing framework like JUnit? The candidate should also have the ability to communicate those results to the proper stakeholders (project managers, executive sponsors, and so on).

Provide Technical Expertise - Provide technical advice and expertise to other technical team members within a project on system architecture, design, and technology alternatives.

Serve as Vendor and End-user Liaison - Serve as the official company representative and contact point for any Web Designer software/platform vendor(s) contacted for technical support. It is often incumbent upon the Web Designer to ensure compliance with Web Designer software vendor on license agreements for the company.

To sum up, a full-charge Web Designer candidate is knowledgeable in installation, project life cycle and methodology, software configuration management, Web Designer security, Web Designer application tuning, troubleshooting, vendor relations, and how to design and code application systems.

Here is a review of the basic knowledge areas for the Web Designer candidate.

Application Tuning

Yet another one of those skill sets that is often more art than science is application tuning. It is almost always a requirement that an application not only be designed to solve a particular business problem, but be able to perform given a certain set of metrics. This often involves negotiating with end users and setting up user agreements and benchmarking requirements.

A successful Web Designer candidate should be able to bring forward and demonstrate tuning strategies they have used in the past that may or may not have worked. Was he or she ever called upon to investigate and resolve performance tuning issues at different levels of the application (i.e., the database, network, host operating system)?

Candidates should be prepared to discuss the pros and cons of Just-In-Time compilers, profiling tools, garbage collection, efficient use of looping, data structures, and algorithms, multithreading, and synchronization.

Troubleshooting

The flair for troubleshooting is a characteristic that is not common to all people. The art of troubleshooting requires an analytical and systematic approach, where the problem is laid out in discrete parts, and each is attacked in a methodical fashion until the problem can be resolved.

A dedicated Web Designer is always available!

Troubleshooting sometimes requires the Web Designer to admit he or she does not know something and must have the wherewithal to look for the answer. In responding to questions about troubleshooting, the Web Designer candidate should be prepared to discuss real-life experiences. The best examples are those illustrating a lot of thought and multiple troubleshooting steps.

Communication Skills

Great technical skills are needed by the Web Designer, but technical knowledge alone does not guarantee job success. As mentioned earlier, a Web Designer needs to be polite when dealing with team members, managers, vendors, and end users. Because a significant percentage of Web Designers' work requires interacting with others on multiple levels, they must be able to speak, think, and write clearly and concisely. A good Web

Designer should strive to set the standard for quality oral and written communication skills.

An inventory of a Web Designer's communication skills starts with the professional résumé. Their résumé should be easy to read and reflect the candidate's publishing and speaking credits. Whether they were a keynote speaker at a national conference or merely presented a topic at a local user group, those experiences document the candidate's communication skills.

The interviewer should bring questions about job experiences that required the candidate to write documentation or procedures. It should be assumed that candidates with an advanced degree, such as a Master's or PhD, have well-developed writing skills, or they would not have reached that level of education. Candidates should be encouraged to bring to the interview their dissertations or other writing samples.

A successful Web Designer absolutely must possess strong verbal communication skills. The ability to listen is just as important as the ability to speak clearly. Their daily routine will include listening to complaints and requests, processing that information, and providing responses and instructions.

Conclusion

In sum, the Web Designer must have a well-rounded skill set, including more than just technical skills. Next, the topics of screening techniques for Web Designers and examine techniques and tools for verifying technical skill will be explored.

Appearances can be deceiving; it's not always possible to easily spot a successful Web Designer.

Conclusion

Initial Screening

CHAPTER 4

Preparation

Thorough preparation and attention to detail during the screening process can save significant amounts of money and resources as well as prevent potentially disastrous problems from ever occurring. Filling vacant positions is expensive, and a careful approach during the initial screening can reap tremendous dividends over time.

Be sure to screen for mental health issues!

In the opinion of many IT managers, an effective Web Designer should have plenty of significant real-world experience to supplement technical knowledge. It has become trendy in the past few years to create sub-categories of job roles, such as Development, Production and Production Support. However, in many large corporations, the Web Designer is the respected technical guru who participates in all phases of system development, from the initial system analysis to the final physical implementation. Hence, the Web Designer generally has significant experience in development and systems analysis.

Troubleshooting skills are essential for the Web Designer.

The High Cost of Attrition and Hiring Overhead

The IT industry suffers from one of the highest attrition rates of all professional jobs. This is due, in part, to the dynamic nature of technology.

An individual may find himself grossly underpaid and decide to market his skills within a relatively short period of time. Someone else may experience a lack of challenge in a job that he or she has successfully performed for some time.

For example, an IT job candidate might enter a shop that needs a great deal of work done, only to stabilize the environment to the point that they are bored most of the time. The IT manager must try to distinguish between the "job hopper" and the individual who is changing jobs solely because of a personal need for more challenging work.

The cost of hiring varies by position and by geographic location, but is rarely less than $10,000 per employee. Filling higher end positions, such as Senior Web Designer/Enterprise Developer, can often exceed $50,000, as specialized headhunters are required to locate the candidate, and these headhunters commonly charge up to 50 percent of the candidate's first-year wages for a successful placement.

There are also the fixed costs of performing background checks and credit checks, as well as HR overhead incurred in checking the individual's transcripts and other résumé information.

Choosing Viable Candidates

While reviewing hundreds of applications for a single job, the IT manager must quickly weed-out "posers" and job candidates who do not know their own limitations.

To be efficient, the IT manager must quickly drill-down and identify the best three or four candidates to invite for an in-depth technical interview by an experienced Web Designer.

Shops that do not currently have a Web Designer on staff generally hire a Web Designer consultant for this task.

Computer consultants are commonly asked to help companies find the best Web Designers for a permanent position.

Later on in this chapter, some of the questions used when evaluating Web Designer candidates for corporate clients are provided.

"Yes, I know C++, J2EE and two other programming words."

Dealing with IT Headhunters

When seeking to fill a top-level IT position such as senior Web Designer, Web Designer enterprise developer, or chief architect, it is not uncommon to employ IT headhunters. These IT headhunters can charge up to 50 percent of the IT job's base salary in return for a successful placement.

However, the aggressive nature of IT headhunters often does a disservice to the IT candidate, and puts the IT manager in a tenuous position. For example, it is not uncommon for the IT manager to receive résumés from two different sources for the same candidate, each represented by different head hunting firms.

In cases like this, it is prudent to immediately remove that candidate from the prospective pool, in order to avoid the inevitable feuding between competing headhunter firms.

When dealing with headhunters, it's also important to get a guarantee that the IT employee will remain in the shop for a period of at least one year and to amortize the payments to the headhunter over that period. Those IT managers who fail to do this may find themselves spending up to $50,000 for a job candidate who quits within ninety days because he or she is not satisfied with their new job.

It's also important to remember to negotiate the rate with the headhunters. While they may typically command anywhere between 20 and 50 percent of the IT employee's first-year gross wages, these terms can often be negotiated prior to extending an offer to the IT candidate. In many cases, this works to the disadvantage of the IT candidate, especially when the headhunter refuses to negotiate the terms, thereby making another candidate more financially desirable for the position.

General Evaluation Criteria

Remember, all Web Designers are not created equal. They range from the entry-level Web Designer to a fully skilled, fire-breathing Web Designer enterprise architect with extensive credentials. What level of Web Designer does the company require? Consider what happens if such a fire-breathing Web Designer is employed in a position that requires only code maintenance of several legacy systems.

That individual will soon grow bored and find fertile application development projects elsewhere. On the other hand, hiring an entry-level Web Designer for a slot that requires tenacity, drive, initiative, and top-shelf troubleshooting skills is begging for disappointment.

Not all Web Designers have equal intelligence.

It is not easy to match the right candidate for a given job. Given the choice between someone who could write an ECommerce system from scratch (but lacked certain personality skills) and a technically inexperienced Web Designer who demonstrates the personality traits mentioned above, the less experienced candidate is frequently the best choice.

The typical entry-level Web Designer usually has a good-looking résumé that is full of projects and jobs involving programming.

However, the interviewer must subtract points if that work involved third-party Integrated Development Environments (IDEs) that were pre-installed and the Web Designer's main duties were simple code maintenance.

When the candidate can't answer in-depth questions concerning the fundamentals of the Web Designer language, the person should be considered to be a "Web Designer newbie" rather than a Web Designer-level candidate. Inexperienced Web Designers often believe their knowledge is more extensive than it really is. In other words they just aren't aware of what they don't know!

Networking skills may be desirable for a Web Designer.

A rule of thumb for hiring Web Designers is to avoid hiring an overqualified person who won't be happy in a job with minimal responsibilities. In a shop that utilizes a third-party Integrated Development Environment (IDE) and relies on pre-configured code generators, an entry-level Web Designer should be hired who can jump into gear whenever required to perform code maintenance.

On the other hand, if a high-powered Web Designer is needed, an inexperienced Web Designer should not be hired, unless that individual clearly demonstrates the motivation for high-end learning and the desire to become a full-fledged Web Designer.

Gleaning Demographics from the Candidate

With the strict privacy laws in the United States, the IT manager must be careful never to ask any questions that are inappropriate or illegal. For example, asking the marital status, the number and age of the children, or the age of the applicant himself may make the IT manager vulnerable to age and sex discrimination lawsuits. Hence, the savvy IT manager should learn to ask appropriate questions that reveal necessary information, while protecting the manager and the company from potential lawsuits.

An IT manager certainly does not want to discriminate against a job applicant, but the demographic aspects nevertheless factor strongly into a hiring decision. For example, the job applicant that has three children less than five years of age may not be happy in an IT position that requires long hours on evenings and weekends.

Don't wind-up in court over an offensive interview question!

Another forbidden consideration is the age of the applicant. If the hiring manager works for a company that guarantees retirement where age plus years of service equals 70, then hiring a 60-year-old candidate could expose the company to paying that candidate a lifetime pension for only a few years of service.

Gleaning Demographics from the Candidate

Mature Web Designers can add spice to the workplace!

Other important demographical information in our highly mobile society is the depth of connection the IT candidate has to the community. Those IT candidates who do not have extended family, close relatives, and long-term relationships in the community may be tempted to leave the position to seek more lucrative opportunities in other geographical areas.

Given that this information can be critical to the hiring decision and at the same time inappropriate to ask directly, the hiring manager may resort to asking somewhat ambiguous questions to get this information. For example, the manager may ask, "What do you do to relax"? This open-ended question will often prompt the candidate to talk about activities they engage in with their families and with the community. Unfortunately in certain situations a simple question such as this could be interpreted as a discriminatory practice. The savvy hiring manager will take care to avoid asking any questions that could be considered the least bit inappropriate. Participating in casual small talk with the applicant before or after the interview can also be viewed as a covert attempt to gather forbidden information. The hiring manager must take care to avoid forbidden topics while interacting with the candidate at any time.

The Selection Process

Generally, the selection of a Web Designer can be accomplished in the following phases:

- Initial screening of résumés by the HR department (keyword scan)
- Non-technical screening by the IT manager (telephone interview)
- In-depth technical assessment by a senior Web Designer
- On-site face-to-face interview (check demeanor, personality, and attitude)
- Background check (verify employment, education, certification)
- Written job offer

Résumé Evaluation

As mentioned earlier, it is not uncommon to receive hundreds of résumés for a particular Web Designer job position. The goal of the IT manager (or HR department) is to filter through this mountain of résumés and identify the most-qualified candidates for the job interview.

The HR department typically performs a quick filtering through a large stack of résumés to narrow the candidates down to a select few, which are in turn presented to the IT manager.

Some résumés may contain anomalies that can reduce the time required for screening. These anomalies are known as "red flags," and indicate that the job candidate might not be appropriate for the position. Such indicators can quickly weed out dozens of candidates, eliminating the need for a more detailed analysis of the résumé, saving company resources.

Résumé Red Flags

There are several important things to look at when scanning a stack of résumés. The following are a short list used by many IT managers:

Unconventional résumé formatting and font - Occasionally, a nice résumé that is done in a professional font may be presented, but with elaborate graphics, sometimes even including photographs and illustrations. In extreme cases, résumés have been known to arrive printed on pink paper scented with expensive perfumes.

Too much information in the résumé - Another red flag is a résumé that tends to specify a great deal of non-technical information. For example, the job candidate may go into great detail about their love of certain sports, hobbies, or religious and social activities. In many cases, these résumés indicate an individual for whom the IT profession is not a great priority.

Puffing insignificant achievements - It is not uncommon for low-end IT positions to attract job candidates who will exaggerate the importance of trivial training. For example, an IT job candidate may proudly list on her résumé that she attended classes on how to use Windows e-mail in the work environment. Of course, trivia within an otherwise nice résumé too often indicates a lack of real technical skill, and the job candidate may be making an effort to obfuscate that fact by simply listing anything that they can think of.

Gaps in employment time - It's important to understand that the technically competent IT professional is always in demand and rarely has any gaps in their employment history. Sometimes, IT professionals misrepresent their work chronology in their résumés. For example, if they are laid off and are job seeking for 90 days, they may not list that 90-day gap of unemployment in order to make themselves seem more attractive. Of course, the start and end dates of each term of employment must be carefully checked by the HR department, and any false indication of this should be grounds for immediate removal from the candidate pool.

Poor grammar and sentence structure - Because the IT industry tends to focus more on technical than verbal skills, candidates with exceptional technical skills may be found, but whose poor writing ability is apparent on their résumés. Short, choppy sentences, incorrect use of verbs, and misspellings can provide a very good idea of the candidate's ability to communicate effectively via e-mail. Remember, the résumé is a carefully crafted and reviewed document. If there are errors in this, it is likely the candidate lacks adequate written communication skills.

Short employment periods — Within the IT industry, it is very rare to be dismissed from a position in less than six months. Even the incompetent IT worker is generally given 90 days before they're put on probation and another 90 days before they are dismissed from the job. Hence, an immediate red flag would be any IT employee whose résumé indicates that they've worked with an employer for less than six months.

"Yes, I was an NCAA Basketball All-star"
Some job candidates may lie!

Evaluating a Web Designer's Training

Scanning résumés involves evaluating for two factors: work history and academic qualifications. Here are some criteria that have been used by major corporations for résumé screening.

Web Designer job candidates used to have only two sources for determining their knowledge: experience and/or Web Designer training classes. Experience speaks for itself and can be judged as to depth and level of experience. However, any training is only as good as what the candidate puts into the training. Candidates might either gain much or comparatively little from the experience of programming instruction, depending on whether they took their "will to learn" and curiosity with them to class.

In order to pass, a candidate will, in almost all cases, need to have had actual experience as a Web Designer and will need to have knowledge from multiple Web Designer references. The tests were developed by over a dozen highly skilled and experienced Web Designer developers and have been certified against hundreds of Web Designer candidates. While obtaining a Web Designer certification from these exams is no absolute guarantee that a candidate is fully qualified, it can be used as an acid test to separate the wheat from the chaff.

"I've been programming for 35 years."

Telephone Screening

After reviewing the available résumés comes the process of selecting a pool of candidates for further telephone screening. The telephone interview is a useful tool for eliminating those candidates whose actual qualities may not quite match their glowing résumés, saving the time and expense of conducting on-site interviews.

The telephone interview may be either unscheduled or prearranged. In either case, the candidate will be less prepared than for the more formal on-site interview. It can quickly become apparent whether he or she is appropriate for the position.

The telephone is the best tool for pre-screening technical skills.

The un-scheduled telephone screening is an opportunity to discover how well the candidate thinks on his feet, and provides insight into his unrehearsed thoughts and feelings. It can also indicate how well the candidate is organized, since the person who must repeatedly search for basic necessary materials and documents at home is unlikely to demonstrate superior efficiency in the work environment.

The interviewer should cover all pertinent areas, with the goal of confirming the qualifications present in the résumé. The candidate should be well informed about those topics that the résumé indicates are areas of proficiency.

The telephone interview will also reveal a great deal about non-technical qualifications. Is the candidate personable and articulate? How well does he or she listen?

From information and impressions gathered from the telephone screening, the IT manager will be able to confidently select the best-qualified candidates for an in-depth technical interview.

Technical Pre-Testing

The job interview questions in this text are deliberately intended to be presented orally. These questions are designed to elicit answers that should indicate a high degree of experience and skill with a specific technology (or a lack of it). Many IT managers will require the job candidate to take an in-depth technical examination.

The technical examination may be given over the Internet, using job-testing sites such as Brain Bench, or they may be paper and pencil tests administered to the candidate before the start of a detailed job interview.

There are important legal ramifications for using these testing methods. Many job candidates who are not selected for an important position may challenge both the scope and validity of the test itself. These challenges have been applied even to nationally known aptitude tests such as the SAT and LSAT exams; IT exams, and language tests such as C++ and C#. These tests may be especially prone to challenge by the disgruntled applicant.

While it is important to do a complete check of all the technical abilities of the IT candidate, it is very important that a manager never cite the failure of one of these exams as the reason for removal from the applicant pool. This is a common technique used by IT managers when they find a particular candidate's knowledge of the field to be insufficient.

For example, in filling a highly competitive IT vacancy, very small things may make the difference between employment or not. In any case, when rejecting a candidate, the IT manager should generally cite something intangible, such as that the individual's job skills do not completely meet the requirements for the position; or a more nebulous answer, such as that the candidate's interpersonal skills will not mesh with the team environment. Remember, specific citation of failure of any tangible IT testing metric may open the company to challenges and lawsuits.

Developing Questions for Interviews

Interview questions should be diligently researched, and the expected answers listed prior to the interview. When open-ended questions are used, the interviewer should have the level of knowledge required to judge the correctness of the answers given by the candidate.

It may not always be possible to identify drug users

The questions should be broken into categories and each should be assigned a point value based on either a scale, such as from 0–5, or according to difficulty. Technically competent personnel should review interview questions for accuracy and applicability.

At the conclusion of the interview, evaluation of technical ability should be based on the results derived using these point values.

In addition, "open-ended" questions should be included, such as "describe the most challenging problem you have solved to date," or "name one programming product that you have developed that you are most proud of". These open-ended questions are designed to allow the Web Designer job candidate to articulate and demonstrate communications skills.

The IT Candidate's Demeanor

During the face-to-face interview, the IT manager can glean a great deal about the personality of the individual simply by observing his or her body language and listening to the candidate speak. In many cases, the IT manager may assess the interview candidate on non-technical criteria, especially the behavior of the candidate when asked pointed questions. Some of these factors regarding demeanor include:

Eye Contact - IT candidates who are unwilling or unable to maintain eye contact with the interviewer may not possess the self confidence and interpersonal skills required to effectively communicate with end users and co-workers.

Fidgeting - IT candidates who are experiencing high anxiety during an interview may cross and uncross their legs, sit uncomfortably, or twiddle their hair while speaking with the IT manager. These involuntary signs of discomfort may indicate that the candidate does not function well in a stressful environment such as a result driven IT shop.

Diction - For those IT positions that require exceptional communication skills, such as working with the end-user community, it may be possible to determine the presence of these abilities in the candidate simply by listening to their responses. For example, careful IT professionals may demonstrate the "lawyer's pause" before answering the question. This pause, of about two seconds, often indicates that the job candidate is thinking carefully and formulating his response before speaking. It may also be possible to assess how articulate the job candidate is by the use of filler words such as "you know," inappropriate pauses, poor diction structure, poor choice of words, and a limited vocabulary.

"What is my long-term career goal? Actually, I want to get your job."

Appropriate Appearance

A Web Designer job candidate who doesn't take the time to put the right foot forward by maintaining proper appearance probably doesn't have the wherewithal to perform adequately on the job.

Clean, appropriate clothing and proper grooming show that the candidate is willing to make the effort to please the employer. Candidates who are sloppy in appearance and mannerisms may bring those characteristics to the job and to their interactions with other members of the company.

Make sure the Web Designer understands proper dress codes.

Savvy Web Designer applicants will adopt the dress of the executive and banking industry for the interview. This attire generally includes:

- Crisp white shirt
- Conservative tie
- Dark suit
- Dark leather shoes
- Neat conservative hairstyle
- Minimal make-up

Developing Questions for Interviews

Proper job interview attire is important.

Conducting the Background Check

As we have repeatedly noted, a candidate's references must always be rigorously checked. Previous employers should be contacted, if possible, to learn about a candidate's past work history. Many people are good at interviewing, but won't necessarily function well in the job.

Because of the explosive growth of the IT industry, fraudulent résumés have become increasingly common. Job candidates have been known to fabricate their college education and the scope of their work experience, smooth over gaps in their employment history, and exaggerate their job skills.

In some cases, job skills may be exaggerated inadvertently, because the job candidate has only a brief exposure to a technology and does not understand their own limitations.

Therefore, it is very important for the HR department to perform a complete background check before forwarding any of these candidates for detailed interviews with the IT manager. These background checks may require the candidate's waiver signature for the release of all medical, criminal, and credit-related records.

The high rate of fraud found in job applications has spawned a new industry of private investigators that, for a fixed fee, will check national databases, revealing any criminal activity on the part of the job candidate, a history of bad credit, and other moral and demographic factors that may be relevant to their suitability for the position.

Conclusion

In sum, while the recession of 2002 has created a shakeout within the lower ranks of Web Designers, IT managers remain committed to retaining their top Web Designer talent, and those Web Designers with specialized skills are still in high demand.

In today's highly volatile work environment, the average Web Designer rarely stays with a single employer for a long period of time.

Competition remains extremely strong for those Web Designer superstars whose skill and background make them indispensable. While some attrition of Web Designers is inevitable, there are many techniques that savvy IT managers can use to retain their top talent.

At this point, it is time to invite the candidate for an on-site interview. The next chapter will cover how to conduct a technical interview to access the candidate's level of technical Web Designer knowledge.

Preparing for the On-site Interview

CHAPTER 5

Choosing the Right Questions

During the on-site interview, the Web Designer needs to be evaluated for both technical skills and non-technical personality traits that will indicate whether the candidate can be successful in the work environment.

Now it's your turn to ask the tough questions!

The specific areas that are chosen to emphasize in the interview will depend on the nature of the position. A system's architect who coordinates the efforts of several people will need a different skill set than someone who primarily works only on code maintenance. Choose questions that will highlight the specific skills needed and look for past experiences that demonstrate those abilities.

An effective Web Designer must be able to wear many hats. He must have the discipline to manage multiple and many times conflicting tasks, the interpersonal skills to communicate with team members and project managers, and most importantly, the technical skills in programming.

This may include, but is not limited to, object-oriented programming techniques, accessing relational databases using JDBC, working with multiple Threads, GUI programming, Perl scripting, Apache maintenance and many other Web Designer fundamentals.

Ask questions that demonstrate these abilities and look for experiences that show accomplishments in these areas.

Questions from the Candidate

Most books and articles neglect to discuss the questions that the candidate may ask the interviewer. This is unfortunate, because whether or not the candidate asks questions and the character of those questions can reveal a lot about his personality and suitability for the job.

After all, the serious candidate will be evaluating the company just as the potential employer is evaluating him. If he is able to ask intelligent questions that are intended to assess how well his particular abilities and goals will integrate with the job, he is actually doing part of the interviewer's job as well.

A certain amount of nervousness is to be expected in the interview process, but the passive candidate who appears reluctant or unable to answer interview questions, as if under cross-examination, can only raise suspicions about the reasons for that reticence.

Contrast this person with the engaging candidate who doesn't answer so much as he conversationally responds, volunteering the pertinent information while interspersing his responses with questions of his own.

The candidate's questions should focus on the tasks and responsibilities he will encounter in performing the job. If the candidate takes the initiative in this way, facilitating the interview as both the candidate and the interviewer explore whether the position is a good fit, chances are he will bring this same constructive approach to the work environment once it is determined that he is indeed, the best person for the job.

Beware of the candidate who only seems to be interested in his salary and the other perks that he will enjoy. There will be time to discuss money once both decide that the alliance is promising.

The thrust of the interview should be on the requirements of the position and whether the candidate is equipped to meet them.

Telephone Pre-interview Questions

At some point in the process, there will be a number of high-quality résumés in the file. Committing to an on-site interview costs time and money for both parties. It is therefore important to consider some pre-interview checking.

Performing a telephone interview to pre-screen geographically remote candidates can help in avoiding travel costs associated with an on-site interview. Also, ask to see their previous work or to contact a former employer. As long as discretion is maintained, this is generally not going to be an issue.

While a quick technical check can be administered over the telephone, it is often performed by a certified Web Designer professional. Questions should be unambiguous, with a clear and accurate answer.

The interviewer should begin by apologizing for asking pointed technical questions before reading each question verbatim. If a candidate asks for clarification or says that he or she does not understand the question, the interviewer re-reads the question.

If the candidate fails to answer a question or answers incorrectly, the interviewer should respond "OK," and move immediately to the next question.

Conclusion

Remember, the only way to accurately evaluate the Web Designer skills of a job applicant is to employ the services of an experienced Web Designer and conduct an in-depth technical interview and skills assessment. For the best results, an experienced Web Designer should administer the interview questions presented in this book.

On-Site Interview Questions

CHAPTER 6

Most Commonly Asked

The following job interview questions are almost universal and most job candidates can expect to discuss these issues during their interview.

1. What are your long-term career goals?

   Expected answer:

   Here we are looking for evidence that the job candidate takes their career seriously and has developed a well-reasoned and realistic career plan.

   Remember, the interviewer will have the candidate's résumé in-hand, so the candidate should never express a grandiose plan that is not reflected in their work and academic history.

   The best job candidate will have a realistic career goal, in-line with their education and circumstances. For example, it might be unrealistic to hear a 35 year-old high school drop-out with 4 small children at home talk about achieving an executive management position, while this might not be unrealistic for a 26 year-old MBA. The best answers might include:

   - I want to push myself to the limit, and I'm finishing Graduate School on evenings and weekends

- I'm taking Internet-based training to improve my accounting skills and I hope to become a CPA someday.

- I'm always trying to improve myself and I don't mind working extra hours to learn a new job skill.

Answer: _____

Comment: _____

2. I need somebody quickly. If you are selected, when could you start?

Expected answer:

This question should be asked with a sense of urgency, making the candidate feel as if they might not get the job unless they "screw" their existing employer by walking-out without notice.

This question will measure the candidate's sense of obligation. If the candidate is willing to walk-out of their existing job without notice, they will probably do the same to you someday.

Regardless of your implied sense of urgency, the employee should say that it would be unfair to just walk-out on their existing boss and that they feel obligated to give two-weeks notice.

Answer: _____

Comment: _____

3. Can we contact your previous employers?

   Expected answer:

   This is a loaded question especially if they believe that the previous employer may not have a glowing recommendation for them.

   In almost all large companies, the Human Resources person is directed only to confirm their job title and dates of employment, and nothing else, so they may be safe.

   Remember, you may not need the candidate's permission to contact your previous employer, and this can be damaging if you can bypass the HR department and speak directly with their supervisor.

   In smaller companies however, the manager-to-manager relationship may be fatal. For example, many managers know that they cannot sue for off-the-record comments and personal opinions.

   For example, instead of saying "Joe did not perform his job well", the manager could simply say "I would not hire him," thereby making it impossible for them to pursue any litigation.

   Answer: _____

   Comment: _____

4. Tell me about a time when you helped improve an employee's poor work performance?

Most Commonly Asked

Expected answer:

This open-ended question gives the candidate a chance to articulate their social and analytical skills.

Because the question deals with the possible hurt feelings of the poor performer, this is a great way to access the tact and finesse of the candidate. Top answers might include:

- I pointed-out the problem in an unemotional and non-threatening way, without attributing any blame to the worker. We then worked together to devise a solution to the performance problem.
- I was especially careful not to hurt their feelings but I was very clear that there was a deficiency that had to be corrected.
- I tried to work with the person to get to the root of the problem and made them feel safe that I was not going to report the poor performance to management.

Answer: _____

Comment: _____

5. How would you compare your verbal skills to your writing skills?

Expected answer:

This question reveals the candidate's subjective judgment of their communications skills.

Of course, the candidate's résumé provides clues into their writing skills, and their oral skills can be inferred by participation on debating teams, college communications courses, and membership in Toastmasters.

Can the candidate comfortably discuss their own shortcomings, or are they the type of person who blames everything on others?

Most people will say that their verbal skills need the most work, but there is no correct answer to this question.

Instead, the purpose of this question is to see if the candidate is forthcoming about the deficiencies and willing to take corrective action.

Best answers might include accurate descriptions of their issues and insights into the proper corrective actions.

Answer: _____

Comment: _____

6. Tell me about how you have handled an unsatisfied customer?

Expected answer:

This open-ended question gives you the change to show how you react under stress. Many candidates have very poor people skills, yet are so unaware of their own deficiencies that they sincerely believe that they are an empathetic person, when in reality they may be withdrawn and nerdish.

The best answer to this question should include references to identifying with the problem, an eagerness to act to correct the problem, and a sincere willingness to help.

- I emphasized with the end-user.

Most Commonly Asked

- I tried to get them satisfaction as quickly as possible.
- I was able to not take the issue personally and kept a professional and sympathetic demeanor.

Answer: _____

Comment: _____

7. What is the description for your ideal job?

Expected answer:

This question is designed to allow the candidate to express their job goals and interest in tangible terms. The answer is not as important as their demeanor.

The best job applicants will not say what they think you want to hear and will feel free to express their personal values as they relate to the workplace.

The best answers to this question will be highly detailed with examples and illustrations of their ideal situation. Some of the best (and most honest) answers might include:

- I want to work in a stress-free environment where everybody has a team spirit and job goals are easily achievable.
- My ideal job would be working in a job where I had total responsibility for an important area so that I could work on my team-building skills.
- My ideal job would be for an employer that valued initiative and gave me the freedom to pursue profitable avenues of the business.

Answer: _____

Comment: _____

8. What questions do you have?

   Expected answer:

   This is the signal for the candidate to show you their insights into the operations of your company.

   The best answers should include references as to how they could maximize your company productivity and they should any avoid mention of company benefits and work environment.

   There is plenty of time to ask those types of questions after you have been offered the job.

   Answer: _____

   Comment: _____

The next chapter will go over those questions that a good job candidate will ask and the following chapter will review inappropriate questions that a candidate should never ask at an initial interview.

What Candidates Always Ask

CHAPTER 7

Two-way Street

A job interview is a two-way street and the candidate should always use the interview opportunity to ask question that may affect their propensity to accept the job offer.

A candidate should never ask questions simply for the sake of banter. Each question they ask should have personal value to them and they should only ask questions when they are invited to do-so by the interviewer. Remember, they are free to conduct their own interview after they have been offered the job!

Regardless of personal interest, there are some questions that every job applicant should ask. These questions show insight into the dynamics of employment and show that they are aware of the pitfalls of poor job opportunities.

1. What is the attrition (turnover) rate?

    This is the single most important question to ask at any job interview. Ideally, you want an employer who values the institutional knowledge of their employees and makes a sincere attempt to keep employees for long periods of time.

2. Why is this job open? Did someone quit?

    This can be a loaded question and you must answer honestly. If the candidate accepts the position and finds out that they are the latest in a string if dissatisfied employees, they may have a legal cause of action against your company for employment fraud.

3. What are my opportunities for advancement?

    This is a great question because it gives you a change to sell the company to a hot candidate. For those candidates who are unlikely to be extended an offer, this is not an important question.

4. Am I expected to work more than 40 hours per week? If so, how many extra hours per week?

    This is a very important question to ask because many employers want to hire young people on a fixed salary and then work them more than 60 hours each week.

5. What are the biggest challenges facing this department?

    This shows that the candidate has a genuine interest in the job and is concerned about their potential to find fulfilling work.

    You should provide an honest assessment of the current situation in your department, the areas of weakness and be very detailed about your expectations regarding the performance of the new employee.

6. What is your timeframe for making a decision?

    This is a legitimate question for every candidate, and one that you will likely hear from the top candidates. Again, an honest answer is appropriate.

What a Candidate Should Never Ask

CHAPTER 8

Best of the Worst

While asking questions is a sign of candidate interest, the candidate should be very careful not to make assumptions and ask inappropriate questions. For example, any savvy job candidate knows that pay and benefits are determined at the time of hire, and the interviewer will not be in a position to discuss specific remuneration items such as pay and vacation time.

They should never assume that they have the job, and should avoid questions that make it appear that they are more interested in compensation than providing value to your company.

Too many questions about company benefits are always in bad taste. They should know that if they are offered the job, they will have an opportunity to review the compensation and benefit packages, and the interview is not the right time to discuss these matters.

Some of the worst questions that I have heard from job candidates include these gems:

1. How often do I get paid?

    This is inappropriate because it indicates financial insecurity. As a general rule, lower wage un-salaried employees are paid weekly or bi-weekly while salaries employees are paid bi-weekly or monthly.

2. Do you offer tuition reimbursement?

   It is never appropriate to discuss benefits and job details until the candidate has been offered the job. If this question comes up, you may say that the details of the compensation will be discussed in detail with the successful candidate.

3. Do you offer paid medical leave?

   This is not only inappropriate but is considered a major red-flag by some hiring managers. Any job candidate who is concerned with such matters may be disguising a serious medical condition.

4. When would I start?

   This question is extremely presumptuous and may indicate a lack of good judgment and tact. All savvy candidates understand that these issues can all be negotiated after an offer is extended.

5. How much paid vacation do I get?

   Again, this is an inappropriate question because the amount of vacation is never known at this stage. You and the HR department have a huge amount of flexibility in offering vacation time, and this figure is often used as a bargaining chip after the job offer has been extended.

6. Is it OK if I take two weeks off before I start?

   Again, this is a presumptuous question and one that is not appropriate for the initial on-site interview.

   Any job candidate who would broach this type of question during an initial interview may have personal issues that may prevent them from performing up to expectations. Further, this candidate may be asking for additional time so that they can take your hiring offer letter to other prospective employers. For obvious reasons, this type of employee should be avoided.

Just for fun

If the interview is going poorly and the job candidate is certain that they would not take the job, they might want to have a bit of fun with you and deliberately ask some job-killer questions.

If the job candidate has self-confidence and wants to see how you react to absurd questions, you may have to handle questions like these.

Some of my favorites include:

1. Do you have an on-site Psychiatrist?

2. Does your company support my Constitutional right to keep and bear arms?

3. What does the company Horoscope predict for next year's earnings?

4. What is your long-term disability plan?

5. Is there a bar near the office?

6. How many warnings to you give before firing employees?

The next step is to review what happens after the job offer has been extended and the candidate evaluates the prospective work environment.

The Job Offer

CHAPTER 9

Negotiations

Once the IT manager has chosen the first candidate, it is common to make an offer based on nationwide studies of the average salaries within the geographical area. For example, IT workers in expensive, professional, urban areas, such as New York City, will earn a great deal more than an IT professional with the same skills, working in a more economical suburban or rural area.

If you decide to make an offer to a candidate, it is a good idea to ask them the salary amount they have in mind. If the candidate is the first to mention a number, the company is placed in an advantageous negotiating position.

If the candidate indicates he or she will be satisfied with an amount that is lower than you were prepared to offer, then you have arrived at the ideal hiring scenario. You have a candidate that you have already decided is desirable for the position, and they will take less money than you had anticipated needing to pay.

On the other hand, if the candidate has an unreasonably high expectation given his skill level and the market in your area, he may have an unrealistic view of the current business environment.

This can indicate that either the candidate didn't do his homework or is simply the victim of wishful thinking. You might point out that the range for this position is somewhat lower than he anticipates. You can then offer the amount you originally had in mind, and negotiate from there.

The knowledgeable IT manager will try to offer a candidate with an excellent set of IT skills a balance between the "going rate" and other intangible benefits, to make the job appealing. Other intangibles might include additional vacation time, flextime, telecommuting, and other perks designed to make the job more attractive to the candidates.

Of course, the savvy IT manager may deliberately reduce the size of the initial offer if he anticipates that the candidate may plan to negotiate for more.

A highly desirable IT candidate may be courted by multiple companies and will often respond to the job offer with a counter offer, citing other employers who are willing to pay more for the same skill set. When this happens, the IT manager may soon be faced with the dilemma of paying more than anticipated for the candidate, and may also question the candidate's motive for earning a high salary.

After the Job Offer

Once the candidate has secured a job offer, the interview process is only half completed. Now they must re-visit the interview process and determine of the job is right for them.

As we discussed, this is the proper time for the candidate to ask detailed questions about their start time, pay, benefits, vacation and work environment.

After the job offer is extended the candidate is in a position to negotiate all aspects of the offer. Of course, pay and benefits are normally hard to change, but adding another week to their vacation can commonly be achieved.

At this point the savvy job candidate will ask the tough questions to determine if the job will be suitable for them. Aside from the obvious issues of pay and benefits, the job candidate is most likely concerned with you, their new supervisor.

Evaluating you!

The candidate's working relationship with you is one of the most important aspects of their job and the single most important factor in their long-term happiness on the job.

We can usually categorize all employees, both managers and workers, into three broad personality areas:

- The Scientist Employee/Supervisor
- The Gung-Ho Employee/supervisor
- The Empathetic Employee/Supervisor

If your personality type is significantly different from the candidate, it does not necessarily mean that the candidate is a bad fit for the job. In many cases a variety of personality types mesh well as a team, off-setting the shortcomings of each type so as to work more successfully together.

However, dissatisfaction with management is one of the top reasons for employee attrition, so the job candidate's final interview before accepting the position should be used to ensure that you will be able to enter a productive and satisfying long-term working relationship with them.

Getting Along on the Job

By themselves, any of these three management personality types do an effective job. However, the problems begin when you have a personality conflict with the candidate.

Find employees with complementary personalities.

There is often conflict between supervisors and employees, and it is interesting to hear employees complain about the shortcomings of their boss. Here is a synopsis of some of the complaints that are commonly heard in the working environment:

Complaints from the Scientist Web Designer

The Scientist Web Designer often enjoys working with an Empathetic supervisor, but has a real problem with the Gung-Ho supervisor.

The Scientist employee feels that the Gung-Ho supervisor is a "loose cannon" and cannot understand their impatience and disregard for detail. Secretly, the Scientist employee thinks that the Gung-Ho supervisor is dangerous, and cringes at their propensity to rush headfirst into everything without proper planning and preparation.

Complaints from the Gung-Ho Web Designer

The Gung-Ho Web Designer sometimes views the Empathetic supervisors as being lax and slow. They may also fault them for having what Mr. Gung-Ho considers skewed priorities (because in many cases the Empathetic supervisors may prioritize family and personal relationships ahead of work).

However, they have a much bigger problem with the Scientist supervisor, whom they see as rigid and overly cautious. Secretly, the Gung-Ho employee thinks that the Scientist supervisor should get moving and stop wasting time proving their theories.

Complaints from the Empathetic Web Designer

Privately, the Empathetic Web Designer does not agree with the high dedication of the Scientist supervisor and the obsessive nature of the Gung-Ho supervisor, but they try to be understanding and are usually hesitant to voice any negative opinions that might hurt someone's feelings. As a result, the empathetic employee tends to absorb unnecessary stress which can accumulate beyond the employee's tolerance level causing a departure in search for a position managed by a compatible supervisor.

Conclusion

Selecting the best Web Designer candidate for the postion is only the beginning of the hiring process. Once an offer has been presented to the chosen candidate, it's the candidate's turn to decide if the job and the working environment are suitable.

The Technical Interview

CHAPTER 10

IMPORTANT NOTE:

The intention of this publication is not to provide a comprehensive technical exam, and the technical questions in this section and the code depot are only intended to be examples. The only way to accurately evaluate the technical skills of a Web Designer job applicant is to employ the services of an experienced person and conduct an in-depth technical interview and skills assessment.

Also note that the expected answers from the questions are highly dependent upon the version of the product and the candidate's interpretation of the question.

We have tried to make the questions as version neutral as possible, but each new release of every product brings hundreds of changes and new features, and these example questions may not be appropriate for your version.

To garner the best results, an experienced technical person should always administer the interview questions presented in this book.

Basic Web Designer Questions

1. Where would you place the most important item on a Web page? (Where is the sweet spot?)

    Skill Level: Low

Expected answer:

> Since people tend to read left to right and top to bottom, they most often look at the upper-left corner first, which makes this an excellent place to put important items. Of course you have to consider your target audience as some cultures do read bottom to top...

Score: _____

Notes: _____

_____

2. How many of the available colors should you use when designing a Web page?

   Skill Level: Low

   Expected answer:

   > It is best to use a limited palette because a simple design is less distracting to the reader.

   Score: _____

   Notes: _____

   _____

3. Name some of the important considerations when choosing colors for a Web design?

   Skill Level: Low

   Expected answer:

   > Does the color convey the right message? Is it true to the theme? Is it readable? Is it comfortable to the eye? Is the level of contrast appropriate? Do the colors match those in the company or product logo?

Score: _____

Notes: _____

_____

4. What other design factors can influence readability of a Web page?

   Skill Level: Low

   Expected answer(s):

   Font size and line length. A small font size can cause eye strain. Long lines of text are harder to read.

   The width of the Web page. While users with larger screens might be able to view your Web page just fine, users with smaller screens may be forced to scroll left and right to view the entire page. One must account for the screen sizes of the target audience.

   Score: _____

   Notes: _____

   _____

5. Can you explain the use of the <blockquote> tag?

   Skill Level: Low

   Expected answer:

   Designers use it to add white space to all sides of a given block of text. It is often used to signify content that has been quoted from another source.

Basic Web Designer Questions

Score: _____

Notes: _____

_____

6. Why is blank space an important part of Web page design?

   Skill Level: Low

   Expected answer:

   It allows the reader's eyes to rest and encourages focus on the important text or images on the page.

   Score: _____

   Notes: _____

   _____

7. Is it appropriate to make entire sentences into links?

   Skill Level: Low

   Expected answer:

   Single word links or small phrases are easier to read and are much less awkward.

   Score: _____

   Notes: _____

   _____

8. What is the tag for a table?

   Skill Level: Low

   Expected answer:

   <table>

Score: _____

Notes: _____

_____

9. What is the tag for a table row?

   Skill Level: Low

   Expected answer:

   <tr>

   Score: _____

   Notes: _____

   _____

10. What is the tag for a table cell?

    Skill Level: Low

    Expected answer:

    <td>

    Score: _____

    Notes: _____

    _____

11. When would you use the *colspan* modifier?

    Skill Level: Low

    Expected answer:

    Use *colspan* to make a table cell in one row stretch horizontally across multiple table cells in adjacent columns.

Basic Web Designer Questions

Score: _____

Notes: _____

_____

12. Describe the use of the *rowspan* modifier.

Skill Level: Low

Expected answer:

It is used to make a table cell in one column stretch vertically across multiple table cells in adjacent rows.

Score: _____

Notes: _____

_____

13. What is RSS?

Skill Level: Low

Expected answer:

Really Simple Syndication (RSS) is an XML-based format for content distribution that is used to syndicate Web content.

Score: _____

Notes: _____

_____

14. What is a CSS?

Skill Level: Low

Expected answer:

> Cascading Style Sheets are remote design sheets that are used to control the appearance of Web pages. Pointing multiple pages to the same CSS simplifies the process of making changes to the format on all the pages simultaneously by modifying the common CSS that defines their appearance.

Score: _____

Notes: _____

_____

15. How can the use of CSS speed the download of Web pages?

    Skill Level: Low

    Expected answer:

    > Using CSS to define the page styles decreases the amount of code in the individual pages making them load faster into the browser. Once the browser loads the CSS one time it no longer has to wait for the design specifications to load for subsequent pages that utilize the same CSS.

    Score: _____

    Notes: _____

    _____

16. How could you move a component from the left to the right side of Web pages that reference a common CSS that uses the CSS positioning attributes?

    Skill Level: Medium

Expected answer:

If you used CSS-P in the original design, you can make a change to the "float" or "position" attributes in the remote design sheet to alter the page. This change would be reflected on every page that referenced the altered design sheet.

Score: _____

Notes: _____

_____

17. What is the W3C?

    Skill Level: Low

    Expected answer:

    The W3C is a consortium that creates Web technology standards such as the specified versions of HTML.

    Score: _____

    Notes: _____

    _____

18. According to the W3C, what is a deprecated attribute?

    Skill Level: Low

    Expected answer:

    A deprecated attribute is one that is outdated due to new developments. Deprecated attributes could eventually become obsolete so should be used with caution.

Score: _____

Notes: _____

_____

19. What is CAPTCHA?

   Skill Level: Low

   Expected answer:

   A Completely Automated Public Turing test used to tell Computers and Humans Apart that was developed by Researchers at Carnegie Mellon University to protect information from automatic retrieval by computers. For example when one does an Internic "WHOIS" search of domain name registrars they are required to read and enter the information from a distorted graphic into a form before accessing the domain records.

Score: _____

Notes: _____

_____

20. What is SSL?

   Skill Level: Low

   Expected answer:

   The Secure Sockets Layer is a point to point protocol that sends encrypted data from one point to another where it is then decrypted for viewing.

Basic Web Designer Questions

Score: _____

Notes: _____

_____

21. What is an IP address?

   Skill Level: Low

   Expected answer:

   An IP address is a 32-bit numeric identifier that is written as four numbers ranging from zero to 255 that are separated by periods. For example, 2.120.11.200 is the correct format of an IP address. An IP address is used to identify a computer or device on a network using the TCP/IP protocol to route messages.

   Score: _____

   Notes: _____

   _____

Section average score: _____

Skill Level: _____

Adobe Photoshop Questions

Use the following questions to evaluate a candidate's skill level in relation to the use of Adobe Photoshop 6.0. /7.0 The following questions are based on beginner to Medium level Adobe Photoshop expertise.

1. What are the steps to create an image?

   Level: Medium

   Expected answer:

   - Select **File>New**
   - Enter a name for the image and specify its dimensions, resolution and color mode.
   - Specify whether to fill the image with **White**, current **Background Color**, or **Transparent**.
   - Select **OK**

   Score: _____

   Notes: _____

   _____

2. What are two ways to browse for an existing file?

   Level: Medium

   Expected answer:

   - Select **File → Browse**
   - Select the folder where the image is located
   - Double-Click on the image you want to open

   Or

- Select Window → File Browser
- Select the folder where the image is located
- Double-Click on the image you want to open

Or

- Select **File** → **Open**
- Select the folder where the image is located
- Double-Click on the image you want to open

Score: _____

Notes: _____

_____

3. Describe how to change an existing image size.

   Level: Medium

   Expected answer:
   - Open the image
   - Select **Image** → **Image Size**
   - Enter the new width and height
   - Select **OK**

   Score: _____

   Notes: _____

   _____

4. What are the steps to show or hide the Tools window?

   Level: Medium

Expected answer:

To show the Tools window, select **Window → Show Tools**

To hide the Tools window, select **Window → Hide Tools**

Score: _____

Notes: _____

_____

5. What is the default file extension of a file saved from Adobe Photoshop?

   Level: Medium

   Expected answer:

   *.PSD, *.PDD

   Score: _____

   Notes: _____

   _____

6. Describe how to enter text on an image.

   Level: Medium

   Expected answer:

   - Open the image
   - Select "**T**" from the **Tools** window
   - Click on the image where you want the text placed
   - Type in the text you want entered on the image

Score: _____

Notes: _____

_____

7. Describe how to check spelling of text entered on an image.

   Level: Medium

   Expected answer:

   After the text is entered choose **Edit → Check Spelling**

   Score: _____

   Notes: _____

   _____

8. What are the steps to crop an image using the **crop** tool?

   Level: Medium

   Expected answer:

   - Open the image you want to crop
   - Click on the **crop** tool from the Tools palette
   - Select the area of the image you want to keep
   - Press enter to crop the image or use an OS shortcut such as in Windows OS, right-click then select crop. Or on the Mac, ctrl+click then select crop.

   Score: _____

   Notes: _____

   _____

9. What are the steps to duplicate an image?

   Level: Medium

   Expected answer:
   - Open the image you want to duplicate
   - Select **Image** → **Duplicate**
   - Enter the name of the duplicated image

   Score: _____
   Notes: _____
   _____

10. How do you create a new layer on an image?

    Level: Medium

    Expected answer:
    - Open the existing image
    - Select **Layer** → **New** → **Layer**
    - Name the Layer (there are also options to indicate a Color, Mode, and Opacity)

    Or
    - Open the existing image
    - Click on the **New Layer** icon in the **Layers** palette

    Score: _____
    Notes: _____
    _____

Adobe Photoshop Questions

11. What does the text feature Type Warping allow a user to do?

    Level: Medium

    Expected answer:

    The Type-Warping feature allows a user to distort type layers in the form of special shapes.

    Score: _____

    Notes: _____

    _____

12. Describe how to select a hidden tool from the tool box.

    Level: Medium

    Expected answer:

    Position pointer on the visible tool and hold down the mouse button until the Tools list appears.
    Select the hidden tool you need.

    Score: _____

    Notes: _____

    _____

13. What are two ways to return a tool or all tools to the default settings?

    Level: Medium

    Expected answer:

    - Select the tool icon on the options bar and choose **Reset Tool** or **Reset All Tools**.

    Or

    - Select Edit → Preferences → General.

- Click on Reset All Tools.

Score: _____

Notes: _____

_____

14. What are the steps to create an audio annotation?

    Level: Medium

    Expected answer:

    - Select the audio annotation tool
    - Enter the options needed such as author's name
    - Click where you want to place the audio annotation.
    - Record message based on the type of operating system.
    - For **Windows** click **Start** then speak into microphone. Click **Stop** to end recording.
    - For **Mac** click **Record** and then speak into microphone. Click **Stop** to end the recording then **Save**.

Score: _____

Notes: _____

_____

15. How is an interpolation method used?

    Level: Medium

Expected answer:

An interpolation method is used to assign color values to any pixels created based on color values of existing pixels in an image.

Score: _____
Notes: _____
_____

16. What does the Channels palette allow a user to do?

    Level: Medium

    Expected answer:

    The **Channel** palette allows a user to create and manage channels and monitor the effects of editing.

    Score: _____
    Notes: _____
    _____

17. What does Masks allow a user to do with an image?

    Level: Medium

    Expected answer:

    Masks allow a user to isolate and protect areas of an image as color changes, filters, or other effects are applied.

    Score: _____
    Notes: _____
    _____

18. Can locked layers be moved or deleted?

   Level: Medium

   Expected answer:

   Locked layers can be moved to a different location within stacking order of the **Layers** palette, but can not be deleted.

   Score: _____

   Notes: _____

   _____

19. How do you merge a layer with the layer beneath it?

   Level: Medium

   Expected answer:

   The layers or layer set must be visible.

   - Select the top layer or layer set of the pair in the **Layers** palette.
   - Choose **Layer → Merge Down** or **Layer → Merge Layer Set**.

   Score: _____

   Notes: _____

   _____

20. How do you create a slice from a layer?

   Level: Medium

   Expected answer:

   - Select a layer in the **Layers** palette

Adobe Photoshop Questions

- Choose **Layer>New Layer Based Slice**

Score: _____

Notes: _____

_____

Section average score: _____

Skill Level: _____

FTP Questions

Use the following questions to evaluate a candidate's skill level in relation to the use of FTP. The following questions are based on knowledge of a typical FTP user who has experience using FTP.

1. For what does the acronym FTP stand?

    Level: Medium

    Expected answer:

    FTP stands for File Transfer Protocol.

    Score: _____

    Notes: _____

    _____

2. What is FTP?

    Level: Medium

    Expected answer:

    FTP is an Internet file transfer service that operates on the Internet and over TCP/IP networks.

    Score: _____

    Notes: _____

    _____

3. What does FTP allow a user to do?

    Level: Medium

    Expected answer:

    FTP allows a user to transfer files over the Internet or a network from one computer to another.

Score: _____

Notes: _____

_____

4. In order to use FTP to transfer files from one computer to another does the user need to have access to each computer?

   Level: Medium

   Expected answer:

   Yes the user must have access to both computers. Typically users may be asked to supply a login and password.

   Score: _____

   Notes: _____

   _____

5. What is Anonymous FTP?

   Level: Medium

   Expected answer:

   Anonymous FTP is used when a user wants to download files from a remote machine but does not have an account. A user who connects to a remote machine as "Anonymous" only has rights to copy files from the remote machine to their local machine but does not have rights to upload files to the remote machine.

   Score: _____

   Notes: _____

   _____

6. When are the files sent to a secure FTP server not secure?

   Level: Medium

   Expected answer:

   Files are not secure after they have been transferred. Unencrypted files are much more vulnerable to being read by unauthorized persons while stored on a publicly-accessible secure FTP server than while being sent to it.

   Score: _____

   Notes: _____

   _____

7. What does the command "**?**" list?

   Level: Medium

   Expected answer:

   The command "**?**" lists a complete list of commands that can be used with FTP.

   Score: _____

   Notes: _____

   _____

8. FTP uses two default TCP connections. One is for **control** and one for **data.** What are they?

   Level: Medium

   Expected answer:

   The default port for **control is port 21** and the default port for **data is port 20.**

Score: _____

Notes: _____

_____

9. What command is used to end a current FTP session?

   Level: Medium

   Expected answer:

   The command **close** is used to end a current FTP session.

   Score: _____

   Notes: _____

   _____

10. Before downloading graphic files or executables what must be typed in the command line?

    Level: Medium

    Expected answer:

    For graphic files or executables type the command **binary.**

    Score: _____

    Notes: _____

    _____

Section average score: _____

Skill Level: _____

JavaScript Questions

Use the following questions to evaluate a candidate's skill level relation to the use of JavaScript. The following questions are based on beginner to Medium level JavaScript expertise.

1. What is a Function in JavaScript?

   Level: Medium

   Expected answer:

   A Function in a JavaScript procedure is a set of statements that performs specific tasks.

   Score: _____
   Notes: _____
   _____

2. What is a String in JavaScript?

   Level: Medium

   Expected answer:

   A String is the characters inside the quotation marks, i.e. document.write("This is a String!")

   Score: _____
   Notes: _____
   _____

3. Does JavaScript need to be compiled?

   Level: Medium

Expected answer:

JavaScript is an interpreted language and does not need to be compiled.

Score: _____

Notes: _____

_____

4. What are the two types of JavaScript?

   Level: Medium

   Expected answer:

   Client Side JavaScript and Server Side JavaScript

   Score: _____

   Notes: _____

   _____

5. What is the correct way to code an alert in JavaScript?

   Level: Medium

   Expected answer:

   alert("This is an alert!")

   Score: _____

   Notes: _____

   _____

6. Inside of which HTML element is the JavaScript entered?

   Level: Medium

Expected answer:

<script> </script>

Score: _____
Notes: _____
_____

7. Where is the correct place to enter JavaScript on an HTML page?

    Level: Medium

    Expected answer:

    A JavaScript can be entered in the Head and Body of an HTML page.

    Score: _____
    Notes: _____
    _____

8. Does an external JavaScript have to contain the <script> tag?

    Level: Medium

    Expected answer:

    No an external JavaScript does not have to contain the <script> tag.

    Score: _____
    Notes: _____
    _____

9. How can you add a comment in JavaScript?

   Level: Medium

   Expected answer:

   /* This is an example of a comment */

   Score: _____
   Notes: _____
   _____

10. How do you code a message in the browsers status bar?

    Level: Medium

    Expected answer:

    defaultStatus = "The is a customized message in status bar"

    Score: _____
    Notes: _____
    _____

11. What is the correct syntax to write "this is JavaScript"?

    Level: Medium

    Expected answer:

    Document.write("this is JavaScript")

    Score: _____
    Notes: _____
    _____

12. How do you insert quotes in strings?

    Level: Medium

    Expected answer:

    Quotes in strings should be preceded by a backslash. This will allow the JavaScript interpreter to distinguish a quote within the string from the quotes that serve as string delimiters.

    Score: _____

    Notes: _____

    _____

13. How do you change a document's background color?

    Level: Medium

    Expected answer:

    To change a document's background color, set the document.bgcolor property to the desired color, i.e. document.bgcolor= "#EFEFEF"

    Score: _____

    Notes: _____

    _____

14. How is form input validated before sending to the server?

    Level: Medium

    Expected answer:

    To validate form input, call your validation function from the form's onSubmit event handler. When the form is submitted, the browser will first run the onSubmit event handler. If the handler returns true, the form will be submitted to the server.

Score: _____

Notes: _____

_____

15. What does the switch/case statement do?

    Level: Medium

    Expected answer:

    The switch/case statement checks a variable against multiple values.

    Score: _____

    Notes: _____

    _____

16. What does the setTimeout command do?

    Level: Medium

    Expected answer:

    The setTimeout command is a way to add a pause to a process.

    Score: _____

    Notes: _____

    _____

17. What does the parseInt method do?

    Level: Medium

Expected answer:
>The parseInt method changes a text string into a number.

Score: _____

Notes: _____

_____

18. What does the toGMTString() method do?

    Level: Medium

    Expected answer:
    >The toGMTString() method converts a date-object to a string with the look of the GMT-Convention.

    Score: _____

    Notes: _____

    _____

19. Can multiple .js files be used in the same HTML document?

    Level: Medium

    Expected answer:
    >Yes

    Score: _____

    Notes: _____

    _____

20. Can a border size of a table be changed dynamically?

    Level: Medium

Expected answer:
Yes

Score: _____

Notes: _____

_____

Section average score: _____

Skill Level: _____

PHP Scripting Questions

1. What is PHP?

   Level: Low

   Expected answer:

   PHP is a server-side scripting language that allows you to submit specifications for Web pages that are executed by the Web server software (such as Apache) before the pages are sent to the requesting browser for display.

   Score: _____

   Notes: _____

   _____

2. Name the variable in the following PHP script and describe how the code is manipulating the variable:

   ```
   1. <?php
   2. $vocal = "you're hired!";
   3. print ("Convince me you are the best person for the
      job and I will say $utterance");
   4. print ("<p>");
   5. $vocal = "you're fired!";
   6. print ("If you screw up I'm going to say $utterance");
   7. ?>
   ```

   Level: Low

   Expected answer:

   The variable "vocal" is created and first set to the value "You're hired!" Then it is reset to the new value "You're fired!" When executed it will display the following two lines of text in the browser:

   ```
   Convince me you are the best person for the job and I
   will say you're hired!

   If you screw up I'm going to say you're fired!
   ```

PHP Scripting Questions

Score: _____

Notes: _____

_____

3. Explain how to use PHP scripting to create a <p> tag in HTML to insert a paragraph break between lines of output from a PHP script?

   Level: Low

   Expected answer:
   ```
   print ("<p>");
   ```

   Score: _____

   Notes: _____

   _____

4. How do you include quotation marks in the output from a print statement?

   Level: Low

   Expected answer:
   ```
   print (" \"Please do it right\"" );
   ```

   Score: _____

   Notes: _____

   _____

5. Compare the difference in the delivery of results when using the "Post" method or the "Get" method to move information from an HTML form to a PHP script.

   Level: Medium

Expected answer:

> The "post" method delivers the information from the form hidden in the background, and the "get" method delivers the results as part of the URL.
>
> Example: http://rampant.cc/cart/log_in.php?UserID=sara&pswd=terrier&submit=Enter

Score: _____

Notes: _____

_____

6. Explain the use of the PHP `array()` function.

   Level: Low

   Expected answer:

   > The `array()` function is used to create a variable to which you assign multiple values.

   Score: _____

   Notes: _____

   _____

7. Give an example using the `array()` function to create and assign values to a simple array.

   Level: Medium

   Expected answer:

   ```
   $girls = array ( "Amy", "Penny", "Linda", "Cindy" );
   ```

   In other words:

   ```
   variable = array ("value", "value", "value", "value" );
   ```

PHP Scripting Questions

Score: _____

Notes: _____

_____

8. List the key numbers used to identify the individual values within the array you described in the answer to question # 6.

   Level: Medium

   Expected answer:

   ```
   $girls[0] = "Amy";
   $girls[1] = "Penny";
   $girls[2] = "Linda";
   $girls[3] = "Cindy";
   ```

   Score: _____

   Notes: _____

   _____

9. Name the two sets of PHP tags that are always available to designate blocks of code within HTML.

   Level: Low

   Expected answer:

   ```
   Standard    <?php    ?>
   Script      <SCRIPT LANGUAGE="php"></SCRIPT>
   ```

   Score: _____

   Notes: _____

   _____

10. List the standard data types that are available for use within PHP.

    Level: Medium

    Expected answer:

    Integer, Double, Array, Boolean, String and Object

    Score: _____

    Notes: _____

    _____

11. How do you declare variables in PHP?

    Level: Low

    Expected answer:

    Variables are not declared in PHP, instead they are prefixed with a $ sign.

    Score: _____

    Notes: _____

    _____

12. Describe the use of the dot (.) operator.

    Level: Low

    Expected answer:

    The dot (.) operator is used to produce string concatenation in PHP.

    Score: _____

    Notes: _____

    _____

13. Explain the use of Counted Loops.

   Level: Medium

   Expected answer:

   You would use counted loops when you want to execute a statement or a list of statements for a predetermined number of repetitions. Do not add a semicolon to the end of the *for* statement. The block of code will be executed only once if a semicolon is added to the end of the *for* statement.

   Score: _____

   Notes: _____

   _____

14. List and describe eight (8) type specifiers.

   Level: Medium

   Expected answer:

   X   Display an integer as an uppercase hexadecimal number (base 16)
   x   Display an integer as a lowercase hexadecimal number (base 16)
   d   Display an argument as a decimal number
   c   Display an integer as an ASCII equivalent
   b   Display an integer as a binary number
   o   Display an integer as an octal number (base 8)
   f   Display an integer as a floating-point number (double)
   s   Display an argument as a string

   Score: _____

   Notes: _____

   _____

15. Explain the use of the nl2br() function.

    Level: Medium

    Expected answer:

    The nl2br() function inserts line breaks into the Web page by turning every new line into a break so as to prevent the text from running together in an awkward lump.

    Score: _____

    Notes: _____
    _____

16. Describe the integer returned by the time () function?

    Level: Medium

    Expected answer:

    It is a timestamp, the number of seconds that have elapsed since the UNIX epoch which was midnight GMT on January 1, 1970.

    Score: _____

    Notes: _____
    _____

17. Explain the $_POST superglobal?

    Level: Medium

    Expected answer:

    It is a built in associative array that holds the values that have been submitted as part of a POST request.

Score: _____

Notes: _____

_____

18. What is a cookie?

Level: Low

Expected answer:

A cookie is a file containing a minimal amount of data that is stored by a Web browser in response to a request from a script or a server. They are often used as a means to identify and track Web site visitors.

Score: _____

Notes: _____

_____

Section average score: _____

Skill Level: _____

Dreamweaver Questions

You can use the following questions to evaluate a candidate's skill level with Dreamweaver. The following questions are based on beginner to Medium level Dreamweaver expertise.

1. Why would you use Design Notes?

   Skill Level: Low

   Expected answer:

   Design Notes can be used to leave notes to yourself about your file that no one else can see because they are stored in a file separate from the source file.

   Score: _____

   Notes: _____

2. What are .png, .gif, and .jpg files?

   Skill Level: Low

   Expected answer:

   These are graphics files.

   Score: _____

   Notes: _____

3. How do you set a title for your page?

   Skill Level: Low

Expected answer:

In the Document toolbar that appears at the top of the Document window:

- type a title for the page in the Title text box, such as Connors Home Page.
- Save the page.

Or

- Select **Modify → Page Properties**. Type the new title in the Title text box and click **OK**. Save the page.\

Score: _____

Notes: _____

_____

4. Explain how to add an image to a Web page?

   Skill Level: Low

   Expected answer:

   To insert images click in the Design view to designate the location where you want the image, then select **Insert → Image**. Save the file.

   Or

   To insert images click in the Design view to designate the location where you want the image, then click the **Insert Image** icon in the Common view of the Objects palette.

   Score: _____

   Notes: _____

5. What is the keyboard shortcut to create a new paragraph (<p>)?

   Skill Level: Low

   Expected answer:

   To create a new paragraph (<p>), press the **RETURN** or **ENTER** key on the keyboard.

   Score: _____

   Notes: _____

   _____

6. What is the keyboard shortcut to create a carriage return (<br>)?

   Skill Level: Low

   Expected answer:

   To create a carriage return (
 ), press **SHIFT** + **RETURN** or **ENTER** on the keyboard.

   Score: _____

   Notes: _____

   _____

7. How do you check for broken links within the current document?

   Skill Level: Low

   Expected answer:

   In the toolbar you would select **File → Check Page → Check Links**, or **File → Check Links**.

Dreamweaver Questions **139**

A Broken Links report will appear in the Link Checker panel.

Score: _____

Notes: _____

_____

8. List the database systems Dreamweaver supports for PHP development?

   Skill Level: Low

   Expected answer:

   Dreamweaver only supports the MySQL database system for PHP development.

   Score: _____

   Notes: _____

   _____

9. What is a URL parameter?

   Skill Level: Medium

   Expected answer:

   URL parameters are name/value pairs attached to URLs. They start with a question mark and include name=value with an ampersand (&) separating multiple URL parameters. For example:

   ```
   http://www.dba-oracle.com/sales/document?name1=value1&name2=value2
   ```

Score: _____

Notes: _____

_____

10. How is a URL parameter created?

    Skill Level: Medium

    Expected answer:

    URL parameters are produced when the `GET` method is used with an HTML form. The parameter value is added to the URL request when the form is submitted using the `GET` method.

    URL parameters can also be created using hyperlinks designed to pass URL parameters.

    For example the following two hyperlinks let the user designate their gender to the server.

    ```
    <a href="http://www.rampant.cc/index.cfm?gender=male">Male</a>
    <a href="http://www.rampant.cc/index.cfm?gender=female">Female</a>
    ```

Score: _____

Notes: _____

_____

11. Explain the use of image re-sampling.

    Skill Level: Medium

Expected answer:

Image re-sampling is used to reduce the size of an image file to decrease the download time period. This reduction is accomplished while increasing or decreasing pixels in a resized image file to make it match the original file's appearance as much as possible.

Score: _____

Notes: _____

_____

12. List three Dreamweaver imaging editing features for .BMP files:

    Skill Level: Medium

    Expected answer:

    Dreamweaver image-editing features do not apply to .bmp files. They can only be used with JPEG and GIF image file formats. The features available for JPEG and GIF image files include Cropping, Re-sampling, Sharpening, Brightness and Contrast.

    Score: _____

    Notes: _____

    _____

13. What folder should be created first before setting up a new site in Dreamweaver.

    Skill level: High

    Expected answer:

    The local root folder

Score: _____

Notes: _____

_____

14. What tool option allows the user to build, delete, or modify sites?

    Skill level: Low

    Expected answer:

    The **Manage Sites** tool option allows the user to build, delete or modify sites.

    Score: _____

    Notes: _____

    _____

15. How many page views are in Dreamweaver and what are they?

    Skill level: Low

    Expected answer:

    There are three page views in Dreamweaver named Code, Design and Split (or combined Code and Design view).

    Score: _____

    Notes: _____

    _____

16. What files do the local and remote views list?

    Skill level: High

Expected answer:

> The local view lists files located on the local machine and the remote view lists files located on a remote machine usually the server.

> Score: _____
> Notes: _____
> _____

17. Describe how to create a table in Design view.

    Skill level: Medium

    Expected answer:

    > Select **Insert** → **Table**, or click the **Insert Table** icon in the Common view of the Objects palette.

    > Choose the number of Rows and Columns (There are also other options there to choose such as Border Thickness, Cell padding and spacing, Header, and Accessibility options).

    > Click **OK** to create the table.

    > Score: _____
    > Notes: _____
    > _____

18. What are some of the basic page templates located in Dreamweaver?

    Skill level: Medium

Expected answer:

The basic page templates in Dreamweaver are HTML, HTML template, Library item, ActionScript, CSS, JavaScript, and XML

Score: _____

Notes: _____

_____

19. When creating a hyperlink in Dreamweaver what Target option must be selected in order for the file to open in a new window?

    Skill level: Low

    Expected answer:

    A new window will open if the Target option is _blank

    Score: _____

    Notes: _____

    _____

20. Describe how to insert a background image on an existing page.

    Skill level: High

    Expected answer:

    - Open the page you to which you want to add a background.
    - Select **Modify** → **Page Properties** and then choose **Appearance.**
    - For **Background image** browse to where the image is located on your computer and select the image.

Dreamweaver Questions

- Select **Apply** or **OK** and **Save**.

Score: _____

Notes: _____

_____

21. What are the steps to view Orphaned Files in Dreamweaver?

    Skill level: Medium

    Expected answer:

    Select **Site → Check Links Sitewide**
    From the **Show** option choose **Orphaned Files**

    Score: _____

    Notes: _____

    _____

22. What does the Site Map view in Dreamweaver display?

    Skill level: Medium

    Expected answer:

    The Site Map view displays the navigational structure of the Web site.

    Score: _____

    Notes: _____

    _____

Section average score: _____

Skill Level: _____

MySQL Questions

1. What is MySQL?

   Skill Level: Low

   Expected answer:

   MySQL is open source relational database software that is often used to create database driven Web sites.

   Score: _____

   Notes: _____

   _____

2. What can you tell me about the MySQL Error log?

   Skill Level: Medium

   Expected answer:

   It logs any errors produced while the server is running, including data from startup and shutdown. It is found in the data directory and includes information about unauthorized passwords, and syntax errors in the configuration file.

   Score: _____

   Notes: _____

   _____

3. What is the function of the MySQL Query log?

   Skill Level: Medium

Expected answer:

    It logs the connections and executed queries. It identifies what queries are being run at specific times and shows what user is logged on, as well as their origination point.

    Score: _____

    Notes: _____

    _____

4. What is the difference between the Binary Update Log and the Update Log?

   Skill Level: Medium

   Expected answer:

       The Binary Update log uses a binary format to store the SQL statements that make changes to the database in the order of execution. The Update Log uses a less compressed format to store the updates to the database.

       Score: _____

       Notes: _____

       _____

5. What is the *mysqlbinlog*?

   Skill Level: Medium

   Expected answer:

       The *mysqlbinlog* is an executable binary that is used to display the contents of the Binary Update Log.

Score: _____
Notes: _____
_____

6. What would you accomplish by using the following syntax?
   mysql> DROP DATABASE test;

   Skill Level: Medium

   Expected answer:

   DROP DATABASE is the command for deleting a database in MySQL.

   Score: _____
   Notes: _____
   _____

7. When does MySQL show the prompt -> instead of `mysql>` on the command line?

   Skill Level: Medium

   Expected answer:

   MySQL shows the prompt -> when it is expecting you to continue adding to your command from the previous line.

   Score: _____
   Notes: _____
   _____

8. What will happen if you type `\c` and press enter while typing a command?

   Skill Level: Medium

Expected answer:

> The command will be cancelled. This is handy if you change your mind or realize you have made an error.

Score: _____

Notes: _____

_____

9. What command do you use to exit MySQL?

   Skill Level: Low

   Expected answer:

   > mysql> quit

   Score: _____

   Notes: _____

   _____

10. How do you delete a MySQL table?

    Skill Level: Medium

    Expected answer:

    > mysql> DROP TABLE <tableName>;

    Score: _____

    Notes: _____

    _____

11. Is MySQL case sensitive?

    Skill Level: High

Expected answer:

When a MySQL server is operating on a Unix-based system it is case sensitive in reference to database and table names, because of the relationship to directories and files in the MySQL data directory.

The other time that MySQL is case sensitive is within a command, the column, table, and other names within a command must be written precisely the same in every occurrence within that command.

Otherwise SQL commands can be typed in either upper or lower case.

Score: _____

Notes: _____

_____

12. How do you remove the contents from a MySQL table?

    Skill Level: Medium

    Expected answer:

    mysql> DELETE FROM <tableName>;

    Score: _____

    Notes: _____

    _____

Section average score: _____

Skill Level: _____

SQL Questions

1. What are the different types of loop structures?

    Skill Level: Low

    Expected answer:

    The correct answers are repeat-until, while and the FOR loop. The candidate should state that a FOR loop iterates a specific number of times, while the repeat-until and while structures iterate according to a variable or Boolean value.

    Score: _____

    Notes: _____

    _____

2. What is the purpose of the GROUP BY statement in SQL?

    Skill Level: Low

    Expected answer:

    The correct answer is that GROUP BY is required after the WHERE clause anytime an SQL statement performs aggregation (sum, min, max).

    Score: _____

    Notes: _____

    _____

3. What is the default ordering of an ORDER BY clause in a SELECT statement?

    Skill Level: Low

    Expected answer: Ascending

Score: _____

Notes: _____

_____

4. You want to group the following set of select returns, what can you group on?

   `max(sum_of_cost), min(sum_of_cost), count(item_no), item_no`

   Skill Level: Medium

   Expected answer:

   The only column that can be grouped on is the "item_no" column, the rest have aggregate functions associated with them.

   Score: _____

   Notes: _____

   _____

5. What is a Cartesian product?

   Skill Level: Low

   Expected answer:

   A Cartesian product is the result of an unrestricted join of two or more tables. The result set of a three table Cartesian product will have x * y * z number of rows where x, y, z correspond to the number of rows in each table involved in the join. This occurs if there is not at least n-1 joins where n is the number of tables in a SELECT.

SQL Questions

Score: _____

Notes: _____

_____

6. You are joining a local and a remote table, the network manager complains about the traffic involved, how can you reduce the network traffic?

   Skill Level: High

   Expected answer:

   Push the processing of the remote data to the remote instance by using a view to pre-select the information for the join. This will result in only the data required for the join being sent across.

   Score: _____

   Notes: _____

   _____

7. What is *explain plan* and how is it used?

   Skill Level: Medium to High

   Expected answer:

   The EXPLAIN PLAN is a tool to tune SQL statements. To use it you must have an *explain_table* generated in the user you are running the explain plan for. This is created using the *utlxplan.sql* script. Once the explain plan table exists, you run the explain plan command giving as its argument the SQL statement to be explained. The *explain_plan* table is then queried to see the execution plan of the statement. Explain plans can also be run using TKPROF.

Score: _____

Notes: _____

_____

Section average score: _____

Skill Level: _____

MS FrontPage Questions

Use the following questions to evaluate a candidate's skill level in relation to the use of Microsoft FrontPage. The following questions are geared toward a beginner to Medium level Microsoft FrontPage user.

1. How can I do a global change on all Web pages?

    Skill level: High

    Expected answer:

    > The candidate may answer that dynamic include pages are ideal for this because the change would only need to be made on the included page and then FrontPage would dynamically insert it at run-time into all participating pages.
    >
    > Within FrontPage, global changes are made using the **Edit → Replace** pull-down menu. This screen has a radio button allowing you to apply the change to the current page, a selected range of pages, or all pages on the Web domain.

    Score: _____
    Notes: _____
    _____

2. Are FrontPage global changes easy to back-out if you make a mistake?

    Skill level: High

    Expected answer:

    > No. The candidate should answer that FrontPage always issues a warning that a multi-page global change is non-recoverable.

Score: _____

Notes: _____

_____

3. How can I connect to a database using FrontPage?

   Skill level: High

   Expected answer:

   The candidate should note that FrontPage is just an HTML generator, so the applicant should state that the database code is embedded inside the HTML, regardless of the tool used to generate the HTML (FrontPage, DreamWeaver).

   Calls to a database can be embedded inside JavaScript or PHP, and the developer embeds database calls inside the code.

   To embed PHP in FrontPage, simple click the "code" button at the bottom of the display window. For Oracle connectivity, the developer should mention Oracle's OCI (Oracle Call Interface).

   Score: _____

   Notes: _____

   _____

4. How can you see all pages with hyperlinks to an open page in FrontPage?

   Skill level: High

Expected answer:

FrontPage contains a **View → Hyperlinks** pull down menu that will change the display mode from page-mode to hyperlink-mode, showing all pages pointing to the open page.

Score: _____

Notes: _____

_____

5. You need to do a collage of text and photographs, staggered on the Web page. What technique would use to implement this?

   Skill level: High

   Expected answer:

   The candidate would likely reply that they would create a table with invisible borders to hold the staggered text and photos.

   Score: _____

   Notes: _____

   _____

6. What are the steps to setting up a new Web using the MS Front Page **One Page Wizard**?

   Skill Level: Low

   Expected answer:

   - Select **File**, **New**, and then **New Page or Web** from the tool bar menu.

- Select **Web Site Templates**
- Specify the location of the new Web site
- Select the **One Page Web wizard** and select **OK**

Score: _____

Notes: _____

_____

7. MS Front Page has three options to view and edit pages in a Web. What are they?

   Skill level: High

   Expected answer:

   Normal
   HTML
   Preview

   Score: _____

   Notes: _____

   _____

8. What is the default home page named in MS Front Page?

   Skill level: High

   Expected answer:

   Index.htm

   Score: _____

   Notes: _____

   _____

MS FrontPage Questions

9. What is the default file extension for MS Front Page pages?

   Skill level: High

   Expected answer:

   .htm

   Score: _____

   Notes: _____

   _____

10. How are pages added in MS Front Page Web Navigation? What is its primary use?

    Skill level: High

    Expected answer:

    Pages are added to Web Navigation by drag and drop functionality in MS Front Page. Navigation is primarily used to organize the Web site structure.

    Score: _____

    Notes: _____

    _____

11. What are MS Front Page extensions?

    Skill level: High

    Expected answer:

    MS Front Page extensions are server side programs that enable Front Page users to utilize the program's special components such as hit counters, form mail, and file upload.

Score: _____

Notes: _____

_____

12. Can a page be edited in Preview page view?

    Skill level: High

    Expected answer:

    A page can not be edited in Preview page view.

    Score: _____

    Notes: _____

    _____

13. Describe how to publish an existing Web using the MS Front Page Publish Web wizard.

    Skill level: High

    Expected answer:

    - Select an existing Web to publish
    - Select **File**, **Publish Web** from the menu bar
    - Specify where the Web will be published
    - Enter **user name** and **password** if necessary
    - You will have an option to publish all contents within Web or just changed pages. Select one
    - Publish Web

    Score: _____

    Notes: _____

MS FrontPage Questions **161**

14. What are the steps to insert an image from a local folder on a computer while in Normal page view?

    Skill level: High

    Expected answer:

    - Select Insert, Picture and then From File
    - Browse for the folder on your pc where the image is located and click on the image
    - Select Insert

    Score: _____

    Notes: _____

    _____

15. To create a hyperlink to a file in Normal page view, select **Insert → Hyperlink** and either select the file in Web or enter the file address. If all users have read access to **file.xls** located remotely in a folder name **Share** on the **Access** server. How would the file address need to be entered in order for all users to open the file via hyperlink after the Web has been published?

    Skill level: High

    Expected answer:

    In order for the file to be viewable by all users via hyperlink, the complete address of the file must be entered:

    `\\Access\Share\file.xls`

    Note: Browsing for the file and selecting it is not a correct answer for this question. If this is done, the hyperlink will map to the file on the local computer and only be viewable when following the hyperlink on that computer.

Score: _____

Notes: _____

_____

Section average score: _____

Skill Level: _____

Flash MX 2004 Questions

Use the following questions to evaluate a candidate's skill level in relation to the use of Flash. The following questions are based on beginner to Medium level Flash expertise.

1. What are files created by Flash commonly called?

   Skill level: Low

   Expected answer:

   Flash files are commonly called movies.

   Score: _____

   Notes: _____

   _____

2. How do you open an existing movie in Windows or Mac operating systems by using the menu?

   Skill level: Low

   Expected answer:

   - Choose File → Open
   - Double-click on the movie's filename to open it

   Score: _____

   Notes: _____

   _____

3. What does the Controller panel allow you to do?

   Skill level: Low

Expected answer:

> The Controller panel allows you to control the playback of movies.

Score: _____

Notes: _____

_____

4. How do you make an animation available for viewing with a Web browser?

    Skill level: Low

    Expected answer:

    > Inserting the animation into an HTML document will make it available for viewing with a web browser.

    Score: _____

    Notes: _____

    _____

5. How do you exit Flash in Windows and/or Mac operating systems?

    Skill level: Low

    Expected answer:

    > Choose **File** then **Exit** (Windows) or choose **Flash** then **Quit** (Mac)

    Score: _____

    Notes: _____

    _____

6. Describe the steps to creating a new folder in Flash.

   Skill level: Low

   Expected answer:
   - Click the **New Folder** button at the bottom of the Library window
   - Type a name that describes the contents of folder
   - Press **Enter** (Windows) or **Return** (Mac)

   Score: _____
   Notes: _____
   _____

7. Explain how to edit an entire text block.

   Skill level: Medium

   Expected answer:

   Choose the **Selection** tool and click text. Flash will then put a selection border around the text. This allows you to modify the text.

   Score: _____
   Notes: _____
   _____

8. What are the steps to hyperlink a text to another source?

   Skill level: Medium

   Expected answer:
   - Select the text
   - Choose **Window → Properties**

- In URL text box, type in the web address or location of the file
- In the **Target** drop-down select a target

Score: _____

Notes: _____

_____

9. Describe how to copy a layer?

   Skill level: Medium

   Expected answer:
   - Click the layer name and select the layer
   - Choose **Edit** → **Timeline** → **Copy Frames**
   - Click the **Insert Layer** button to create a new layer
   - Choose the **New layer** to make it active
   - Choose **Edit** → **Timeline** → **Paste Frames**

Score: _____

Notes: _____

_____

10. Describe how to create a self-playing movie on Windows and/or Mac operating systems.

    Skill level: High

    Expected answer:
    - Choose **File**, then **Publish Settings** to open the Publish Settings dialog box

- On Formats tab, mark **Windows Projector** or **Macintosh Projector** check boxes
- Click **Publish**
- Choose **OK** or **Cancel** to close the **Publish Settings** dialog box

Score: _____

Notes: _____

_____

Section average score: _____

Skill Level: _____

Perl Script Questions

Use the following questions to evaluate a candidate's skill level using Perl. The following questions are based on beginner to Medium level Perl expertise.

1. For what do the letters P.E.R.L stand?

    Skill level: Low

    Expected answer:

    Practical Extraction and Report Language

    Score: _____
    Notes: _____
    _____

2. Can Perl run on Macintosh and OS2 operating systems?

    Skill level: Low

    Expected answer:

    Yes

    Score: _____
    Notes: _____
    _____

3. Does Perl need to be compiled?

    Skill level: Low

    Expected answer:

    Yes, Perl needs to be compiled.

Score: _____
Notes: _____
_____

4. What command is entered in the UNIX command line in order to determine if Perl is installed on PC?

   Skill level: Low

   Expected answer:

   perl –v

   Score: _____
   Notes: _____
   _____

5. What are the steps to create a new program in MacPerl?

   Skill level: Medium

   Expected answer:
   - Select File → New → Enter
   - Edit your program
   - Select File → Save

   Score: _____
   Notes: _____
   _____

6. What is a file handle?

   Skill level: Low

Expected answer:

> A handle is a name used in a program to talk about a file. The general rule is to make them all upper-case.

Score: _____

Notes: _____

_____

7. Does Perl have a string length limit?

   Skill level: Low

   Expected answer:

   > Perl string lengths are only limited by the amount of memory that is available.

   Score: _____

   Notes: _____

   _____

8. What are the two functions for opening and closing a database?

   Skill level: Low

   Expected answer:

   > **dbmopen** is for opening a database and **dbmclose** is for closing a database.

   Score: _____

   Notes: _____

   _____

9. What three arguments does the **dbmopen** function require?

   Skill level: Medium

   Expected answer:

   The three arguments of the **dbmopen** function are the name of the hash, the name of the database on disk and the mode.

   Score: _____

   Notes: _____

   _____

10. What is mode?

    Skill level: Low

    Expected answer:

    The mode is the numeric UNIX file mode in which you want to open the file.

    Score: _____

    Notes: _____

    _____

11. What information do you receive from the following? #!/usr/bin/perl

    Skill level: Low

    Expected answer:

    This tells you where Perl is located on your web server.

Score: _____

Notes: _____

_____

12. When saving your Perl script how can you be certain you will get the desired file extension?

    Skill level: Medium

    Expected answer:

    Place the filename including the desired extension in quotes before saving the file. For example: "pedigree.cgi" If you fail to use the quotes your file may be saved as pedigree.cgi.txt

    Score: _____

    Notes: _____

    _____

13. How do you use the –d switch?

    Skill level: Medium

    Expected answer:

    You can use the –d switch to debug a Perl script via telnet. For example, using the following command line will display the first line of the script named "pedigree" for debugging.

    ```
    Telnet/cgi-bin>perl -d pedigree.cgi
    ```

    Type **s** and press **Enter** to go through each step of the script. When finished type **q** and press **Enter** to quit.

Perl Script Questions **173**

Score: _____

Notes: _____

_____

14. Explain how to run the following script in a browser and describe the results:

```
#!/usr/bin/perl

print "Content-type: text/html\n\n";
print "<HTML><HEAD>";
print "<TITLE>CGI pedigree</TITLE>";
print "</HEAD>";
print "<BODY><H3>For pedigree information please email pedigrees@horseinfo.com </H3>";
print "</BODY></HTML>";
```

Skill level: Medium

Expected answer:

To run the script in a browser you would enter the URL of the script in the browser address window.

This script will produce a web page that reads, "For pedigree information please email pedigrees@horseinfo.com."

Score: _____

Notes: _____

_____

Section average score: _____

Skill Level: _____

Apache Questions

Not all Web Designer candidates will have in-depth knowledge of the Apache software but most should at least be familiar with the basic concepts.

1. On what type of server would you most likely find Apache code?

   Skill level: Low

   Expected answer:

   Even a novice knows that Apache is designed for Web server components. Any responses that refer to application server components are incorrect and the candidate should clearly state that Apache is designed for Web servers.

   Score: _____

   Notes: _____

   _____

2. What is a scoreboard?

   Skill level: Medium

   Expected answer:

   The scoreboard in Apache stores the current state of all UNIX processes (and threads within processes for Apache 3.). The scoreboard allows the Apache *mod_status* function to present an overview of the server process and load status.

Score: _____

Notes: _____

_____

3. How would you program Apache to pass user and password information to a back-end database or LDAP server?

   Skill level: High

   Expected answer:

   The candidate should refer to the Apache Authentication Modules. Apache has authentication modules for communicating with Oracle, MySQL and other relational databases.

   Score: _____

   Notes: _____

   _____

4. Explain how you could implement performance load balancing within an Apache Process?

   Skill level: High

   Expected answer:

   The candidate should mention of the use of load balancing modules including *mod_rewrite, reverse proxy, mod_backhand* or *mod_bandwidth* or *mod_throttle*.

   Score: _____

   Notes: _____

   _____

5. Name some common procedural languages that allow integration with Apache. What are the most popular?

   Skill level: Medium

   Expected answer:

   The candidate should mention that PHP is widely used, along with Perl (using the *mod_perl* module). Also, Java (the *mod_jk* module), Python, Tcl, ASP and .NET are acceptable answers.

   Score: _____
   Notes: _____
   _____

Section average score: _____

Skill Level: _____

Security Questions

Security, always an important part of network administration, has gained much publicity in the last few years, as network attacks have become more prevalent and more publicized. The important thing to look for when interviewing a Web Designer candidate is their attitude towards security. Practical knowledge is important, of course, but the truly high level Web Designer understands that security is a process, not a product. Security must permeate everything that happens on the network, from adding and removing hosts to troubleshooting routing problems. Only by placing security as the number one priority will the Web Designer be able to ensure the reliability and availability of the web site. Specifically, their response to question 11 will give great insights into what role security plays in their mind.

1. What issues are involved with operating a packet sniffer on a switched Ethernet network?

    Skill level: Medium

    Expected answer:

    Since a system connected to a switched Ethernet network will only see traffic originating from it, destined for it, or broadcast traffic, a packet sniffer isn't as useful as it is on a shared Ethernet network. In order to utilize a sniffer to its fullest potential, you must designate a port on one of the backbone switches as a management port. This will instruct the switch to copy all traffic to this port, regardless of the source or destination address. When you connect your packet sniffer to this port, all Ethernet traffic will be seen.

Score: _____

Notes: _____
_____

2. You have a Cisco router connecting your LAN to the Internet and you are utilizing the built in firewall capabilities of the Cisco IOS. If a packet traverses your firewall rules and does not match any of them, how does the IOS treat that packet?

   Skill level: Medium

   Expected answer:

   > The Cisco IOS will drop the packet. Cisco always implements an "implicit deny" after all firewall rules, meaning that any packet not matching any rule is dropped. In order to reverse this behavior, you must have a firewall rule (normally the last one) that implicitly allows a packet.

   Score: _____

   Notes: _____
   _____

3. Discuss the pros and cons of stateless and stateful firewalls.

   Skill level: High

   Expected answer:

   > Stateless firewalls require much less overhead, and introduce less latency into the network. They examine each packet individually, with no thought to the packet's relationship to other packets.
   >
   > Stateful firewalls will take into account the fact that a packet is part of a larger data "conversation," and can

Security Questions **179**

make better decisions on what traffic to allow or deny. This comes at the cost of added complexity in setup and greater latency in the network.

Score: _____

Notes: _____

_____

4. What is source-address verification, and why is it an important part of firewall implementation?

   Skill level: Medium

   Expected answer:

   Source-address verification is the process of monitoring all outbound data at a network endpoint, and only allowing data out of the network if the source address matches the subnet from which the data originated. This effectively eliminates "source address spoofing," a common tactic used in denial of service attacks when an attacker is attempting to mask the source of their packets. If this kind of egress filtering was done on all networks on the Internet, the amount of denial of service attacks would be greatly reduced.

   Score: _____

   Notes: _____

   _____

5. What is a DMZ and why is it important?

   Skill level: Low

Expected answer:

DMZ stands for "demilitarized zone." It is a term borrowed from the military that refers to a separate network setup between a company's private network and the public Internet. If a company needs to allow Internet access to a service, that service will run on a host in the DMZ. This 'buffer zone' is desirable because if a system in the DMZ is compromised, an attacker still has no access to the company's private network.

Score: _____

Notes: _____

_____

6. Define and describe a VPN.

   Skill level: Low

   Expected answer:

   VPN stands for Virtual Private Network. Using encryption software, it is possible to setup a secure, encrypted 'tunnel' between two points on a public network (like the Internet). Once this link is established, those two points form a virtual private network, allowing secure communication to take place over an insecure medium.

   Score: _____

   Notes: _____

   _____

7. Define and describe the two main types of VPNs in use on the Internet today.

   Skill level: Medium

Expected answer:

PPTP VPNs are based on the Point-to-Point Tunneling Protocol. This protocol is backed by a coalition of vendors, headed by Microsoft. Client and server software packages to implement this VPN solution are included with versions of Windows after Windows 98 OSR2.

IPSec based VPNs are commonly implemented in hardware VPN solutions from companies like Cisco. IPsec supports two security schemes: Authentication Header (AH), which authenticates the sender of the data; and Encapsulating Security Payload (ESP), which supports sender authentication and payload encryption.

Score: _____

Notes: _____

_____

8. Define the private IPv4 subnets, and explain their importance to the security of a network.

   Skill level: Medium

   Expected answer:

   In order to allow for easy adoption of TCP/IP inside corporate networks, without the possibility of address conflict with the Internet, private IP subnets were created. These ranges of IP addresses are non-routable, meaning they are not valid on the Internet.

   - Class A private IP range: 10.0.0.0 – 10.255.255.255
   - Class B private IP range: 172.16.0.0 – 172.31.0.0
   - Class C private IP range: 192.168.0.0 – 192.168.255.255

Adopting a private IP address space is recommended for a corporate network. This prevents any system on the Internet from directly addressing any internal system. Internal systems are granted outside access by means of Network Address Translation or a proxy server.

Score: _____

Notes: _____

_____

9. Define NAT and describe the benefits.

   Skill level: Low

   Expected answer:

   NAT (Network Address Translation) is used most often in conjunction with a private IP subnet, a system running NAT will forward packets from one network to another, making all source packets appear as if they originate from the NAT system itself. When a reply is received, the reverse happens, with the NAT system rewriting the destination address to allow the packet to be delivered to the requester. This proxying of packets is an important security practice. It also allows a large number of systems to access an outside network through a single IP address.

   Score: _____

   Notes: _____

   _____

10. Describe SSL and trusted third-party Certificate Authorities.

    Skill level: High

Expected answer:

SSL (Secure Sockets Layer) was developed by Netscape to address the insecurities of HTTP communication. SSL is a protocol that allows for the encryption of HTTP sessions using key-based cryptography.

On the Internet, there is little in place to prove that someone is who they say they are. Just because you can make an encrypted connection to someone's online Web store, that doesn't mean that they are a legitimate business. The business of Certificate Authorities has arisen to aid in authenticating these transactions. When a business purchases a certificate from a trusted Certificate Authority (like Verisign or Thawte Consulting), that certificate is presented to every Web browser that attempts to make a secure connection to the business' Web site. If the Web browser trusts the third party Certificate Authority, the connection is allowed. If not, the connection is denied. A list of the major Certificate Authorities is included with the major Web browsers. The analogy for this connection is "I don't trust you, but I trust Verisign, and they tell me that you are who you say you are."

Score: _____

Notes: _____

_____

11. What is the weakest point in every network?

Skill level: Medium

Expected answer:

People. Regardless of how good your firewall, intrusion detection systems, audits and personnel are, your employees will always be the weakest link in your network.

Social engineering is a common way to attempt to exploit the people in a networking environment. Why should a cracker spend days attempting a brute force attack to discover a password, when he can call up a secretary, impersonate someone from the IT department, and get her to give him her password?

Every security policy should include basic security principals for every employee, such as:

- Never give your password out over the phone or in email.
- Challenge any suspicious person you see in the office, etc.

Score: _____

Notes: _____

_____

12. What is a smurf attack, and how can it be prevented?

Skill level: High

Expected answer:

A smurf attack is a term for a common denial of service attack utilizing ICMP packets. An attacker will craft an ICMP echo packet appearing to originate from the victim's IP address. This packet will be sent to the broadcast address of another network. Since packets sent to a broadcast address are accepted by every system on a subnet, and since the standard response to an echo request is an echo reply, the victim soon finds his IP address flooded with ICMP echo replies from this network.

The recommended way to thwart this kind of attack is to block access to broadcast addresses at each network's router.

Score: _____

Notes: _____

_____

13. What is a SYN flood, and how can it be prevented?

    Skill level: High

    Expected answer:

    All TCP connections begin with a three-way handshake. This handshake consists of a SYN from the source, a SYN-ACK reply from the destination, and an ACK from the source. When a system receives a SYN packet, it allocates memory space to handle the connection, sends the SYN-ACK, and waits for the final ACK before communication can occur. This is what is known as a half-open connection.

    A SYN flood occurs when an attacker sends a large amount of SYN requests to a system, spoofing the source IP address of the packets. This will cause the victim's system to send SYN-ACKs to systems that weren't expecting them, and will therefore not reply. As the spoofed packets continue to come in, the victim's system will continue to allocate memory to handle these half-open connections until eventually the memory of the system is exhausted and no more incoming connections are accepted.

There is currently no generally accepted solution for handling this kind of problem because it utilizes the very nature of TCP communication as opposed to exploiting vulnerability. The recommended solution is for originating networks to perform source-address verification on all outgoing packets, eliminating the possibility of a system on their network sending out packets with spoofed IP addresses.

Score: _____

Notes: _____

_____

Section average score: _____

Skill Level: _____

Java and J2EE Versions

Several of the expected answers from these questions may be highly dependent upon the version of Java and the J2EE specification. While we have made every effort to make the questions as version neutral as possible, each release of the J2EE specification brings many changes and new features, and these example questions may not be appropriate for your version of Java/J2EE implementation. As a reference when determining whether behavior and syntax is correct, we use Sun's J2EE 1.3 platform specification.

Qualifications

1. Do you have any Certifications? (i.e. Java Programmer/Developer, Cisco, Microsoft, Oracle)

    Answer: _____
    Comment: _____
    _____

2. What relational database systems are you most familiar with? (Oracle, SQL Server, MySQL, Postgres, etc.)

    Answer: _____
    Comment: _____
    _____

3. What J2EE Application Servers are you most familiar with? (Oracle9*i*AS, OC4J, BEA WebLogic Server, IBM WebSphere, JBoss, etc.)

Answer: _____

Comment: _____

_____

4. Which Java Development IDE are you most comfortable with? (JBuilder, IntelliJ IDEA, JDeveloper, plain 'ol Emacs, etc.)

Answer: _____

Comment: _____

_____

5. Which version control systems have you used in the past? (CVS, Oracle Software Configuration Management, Continuus, ClearCase, etc.)

Answer: _____

Comment: _____

_____

6. Highest level of education?

Most candidates in this field acquire a college education, preferably a BS in computer science, computer information technology or related engineering field.

Answer: _____

Comment: _____

_____

Section average score: _____
Skill Level: _____

Java and J2EE Versions

Java Interview Questions

1. How many public classes are permitted within a single Java class file?

   Skill Level: Low

   Expected answer:

   You can only define one public class within a single Java class file.

   Score: _____
   Notes: _____
   _____

2. How many package statements (declarations) are allowed in a Java source file?

   Skill Level: Low

   Expected answer: Only one.

   Score: _____
   Notes: _____
   _____

3. Is it necessary to have a package statement in a Java source file?

   Skill Level: Low

   Expected answer: No.

Score: _____

Notes: _____

_____

4. In a Java source file, which statement needs to be first, import or package?

   Skill Level: Low

   Expected answer:

   The package statement must come before any import statements.

   Score: _____

   Notes: _____

   _____

5. If all three statement elements of a Java source file are included (imports, classes, packages), in which order must they appear?

   Skill Level: Low

   Expected answer:

   Package declaration, imports, and then all classes.

   Score: _____

   Notes: _____

   _____

6. Consider a program that imports a large number of classes. Is there any performance degradation from importing many classes at runtime?

   Skill Level: Low

   Expected answer:

   No. The import statements only provide the compiler with class name abbreviations and have no performance impact at runtime.

   Score: _____

   Notes: _____

   _____

7. What is the command-line utility used to compile Java source code into bytecode?

   Skill Level: Low

   Expected answer:

   The command-line utility is javac.

   Score: _____

   Notes: _____

   _____

8. What is the name of the method the JVM uses as the normal entry point for a Java application? What is its signature?

   Skill Level: Low

   Expected answer:

   The name of the method is main(). The signature for main() is:

```
public static void main(String[] args)
```

Score: _____

Notes: _____

_____

9. Is it a requirement that the `main()` method be declared as static? Explain why or why not?

   Skill Level: Low

   Expected answer:

   Yes, it is a requirement that the `main()` method be declared static. This is necessary so it can be invoked without having to construct an instance of the corresponding class.

   Score: _____

   Notes: _____

   _____

10. What are the four signed integral data types in Java? What are their sizes and range of values?

    Skill Level: Low

    Expected answer:

Data Type	Size	Minimum	Maximum
Byte	8 bits	-2^7	$-2^7 - 1$
Short	16 bits	-2^{15}	$-2^{15} - 1$
Int	32 bits	-2^{31}	$-2^{31} - 1$
Long	64 bits	-2^{63}	$-2^{63} - 1$

Java Interview Questions

Score: _____

Notes: _____

_____

11. Within your Java application, you catch all exceptions and want to know the exact circumstances under which they occurred. Which method would you use from the throw able class to obtain a complete stack trace?

    Skill Level: Low

    Expected answer:

    You can get a stack trace from any exception object with the printStackTrace() method in the throw able class.

    Score: _____

    Notes: _____

    _____

12. What is the difference between System.out.println() and System.out.print ()?

    Skill Level: Low

    Expected answer:

    The println() method is used to display a line of text that ends with a newline character. The newline character causes the next line of text to begin displaying at the left-most edge of the next line, similar to the carriage return key on a manual typewriter. The print () method, on the other hand, does not add the newline character to the end of the line. This allows you to use several print() statements to display information on the same line.

Score: _____

Notes: _____

_____

13. When creating a `String` object, is it necessary to use the `new` operator?

    Skill Level: Low

    Expected answer:

    No. Java does not require you to use the new operator when constructing a new `String` object. In fact, it is more efficient than explicitly calling the constructor.

    Score: _____

    Notes: _____

    _____

14. What is the value at which a String is automatically initialized?

    Skill Level: Low

    Expected answer: null.

    Score: _____

    Notes: _____

    _____

15. How do you make a variable a constant?

    Skill Level: Low

    Expected answer:

    Declare the variable using the final keyword.

Score: _____

Notes: _____
_____

16. What does putting the + operator between two strings do?

    Skill Level: Low

    Expected answer:

    It concatenates the two strings together.

    Score: _____

    Notes: _____
    _____

17. What characters can be legally used as the first character of a Java identifier?

    Skill Level: Low

    Expected answer:

    Any letter, the dollar sign ($), or an underscore.

    Score: _____

    Notes: _____
    _____

18. What statement would you use to convert the String `str1` to an integer named `int1`?

    Skill Level: Low

    Expected answer:
    ```
    int int1 = Integer.parseInt(str1);
    ```

Score: _____

Notes: _____

_____

19. What statement would you use to convert the String `str1` to a byte named `byte1`?

    Skill Level: Low

    Expected answer:
    ```
    byte byte1 = Byte.parseByte(str1);
    ```

    Score: _____

    Notes: _____

    _____

20. What statement would you use to convert the String `str1` to a long named `long1`?

    Skill Level: Low

    Expected answer:
    ```
    long long1 = Long.parseLong(str1);
    ```

    Score: _____

    Notes: _____

    _____

Section average score: _____

Skill Level: _____

J2EE Telephone Pre-interview Questions

At some point in the process, you will be faced with a number of high quality resumes in your file. Committing to an on-site interview costs time and money for both parties. It is therefore important to consider some pre-interview checking. Performing a telephone interview to pre-screen geographically remote candidates can help in avoiding travel costs associated with an on-site interview. Also, ask to see their previous work or contact a former employer. As long as you remain discrete this is generally not going to cause any problems for the candidate.

The following ten questions should help in determining the technical skill set of any potential J2EE candidate. The questions are simple enough that any qualified J2EE professional should be able to answer them immediately from memory. Any candidate who has a hard time with these questions may not be appropriate for a full time position as a J2EE Developer or Architect.

1. When working with a web application, what is the filename of the deployment descriptor and where should be it located?

    Skill Level: Low

    Expected answer:

    The name of the deployment descriptor for web applications is named web.xml and is typically located in the (web-app-root)/web-INF/web.xml.

    Score: _____
    Notes: _____
    _____

2. What is the name of the XML root element within the web deployment descriptor file; web.xml?

   Skill Level: Low

   Expected answer:

   The name of the XML root element is <web-app>.

   Score: _____

   Notes: _____

   _____

3. What are the two J2EE Web-based technologies that support dynamic content generation of Web pages in a portable and cross-platform manner?

   Skill Level: Low

   Expected answer:

   JavaServer Pages (JSP) and Servlets.

   Score: _____

   Notes: _____

   _____

4. You have a client application that needs to look-up the home interface of an enterprise bean. Which class and method is used to look-up the bean?

   Skill Level: Low

   Expected answer:

   The application would need to use the lookup() method of the InitialContext class, found in the JNDI package. In order to access an enterprise bean, the application will use the JNDI package to obtain a directory connection to a beans container. Once the connection is established, a new InitialContext object is created. The lookup() method of the InitialContext object is then used to look up the bean. The lookup() method will return a reference to the home object of the bean.

Score: _____

Notes: _____

_____

5. What are the two ways in which an *entity bean* can persist enterprise data?

   Skill Level: Low

   Expected answer:

   An entity can use either container-managed persistence (CMP) or bean-managed persistence. With CMP, the EJB container is responsible for handling the implementation of code (SQL) necessary to insert, read, and update an object in a data source. With BMP, the application developer needs to create the implementation code for the insert, read, and update of an object.

   Score: _____

   Notes: _____

   _____

6. You have an application that uses Java objects exclusively. Which distributed technology should you consider for communication; RMI or CORBA? Why?

   Skill Level: Low

Expected answer:

If you have an application that only contains Java objects, it would be appropriate to use RMI. The RMI technology is built right into the Java language as a means of allowing objects to communicate with other objects that are running on JVMs on remote machine within the network. Using CORBA technology, objects that are exported with CORBA can be accessed by clients implemented in any language (C, Perl, etc) with an IDL binding. Although CORBA is more extensive than RMI, RMI is more straightforward to use since it only used Java objects.

Score: _____

Notes: _____

_____

7. You are about the write a *Session Bean*. What are the three types of component (classes and interfaces) that are needed to write a Session Bean?

Skill Level: Low

Expected answer:

To write a session bean, you will need to create the following:

- Home Interface
- Remote Interface
- The actual bean class which implements the SessionBean Interface

Score: _____

Notes: _____

_____

8. Suppose you have an HTTP servlet that overrides the doGet() method for receiving GET requests. What are the names of the two classes passed into the doGet() method that will allow you to receive requests and to respond to the Web client?

   Skill Level: Low

   Expected answer:

   The two object types are HttpServletRequest and HttpServletResponse. The HttpServletRequest object represents the client's request and provides the servlet with access to information about the client, the parameters for the request, and the HTTP headers passed along with the request. The HttpServletResponse object represents the servlet's response and is used to return data to the client.

   Here is the signature of an example doGet() method:

   ```
   public void doGet(
     HttpServletRequest req
   , HttpServletResponse res
   )
   throws ServletException, IOException {}
   ```

   Score: _____

   Notes: _____

   _____

9. Given an HTTP PUT method, what is the corresponding method in the HttpServlet class that will be called upon invocation?

   Skill Level: Low

Expected answer:

The doPut() method. The doPut() method of the HttpServlet abstract class is used to handle the HTTP PUT type request.

Score: _____

Notes: _____

_____

10. In a Java Server Page (JSP), how would you declare a String object named firstName and assign it the value of "*Sara*"?

Skill Level: Low

Expected answer:

<%! String firstName = new String("Sara"); %>

Score: _____

Notes: _____

_____

Section average score: _____

Skill Level: _____

J2EE Development Concepts

1. A J2EE application is divided into components based on the function they need to support. What are the components defined in the J2EE specification?

   Skill Level: Low

   Expected answer:

   Application clients and applets are components that run on the client machine.

   Score: _____

   Notes: _____

   _____

2. Java Servlets and JavaServer Pages (JSP) are Web-based components that run within a Web container on the server.

   Skill Level: Low

   Expected answer:

   Enterprise JavaBeans (EJB) components (also known as enterprise beans) are business components that are run within an EJB container on the server.

   Score: _____

   Notes: _____

   _____

3. What is the Remote Method Invocation (RMI) Protocol?

   Skill Level: Medium

Expected answer:

Remote Method Invocation (RMI) is a set of APIs that allows developers to build distributed applications using the Java programming language. Defined in the Java language, RMI uses interfaces to define remote objects with a combination of Java serialization and the Java Remote Method Protocol (JRMP) to turn local method invocations into remote method invocation.

Score: _____

Notes: _____

4. What is the Java Remote Method Protocol (JRMP)?

   Skill Level: High

   Expected answer:

   Java Remote Method Protocol (JRMP) is a proprietary wire-level protocol designed by Sun Microsystems to support the transparent mechanism required for communication between objects in the Java language that reside in different address spaces. The J2EE supports the JRMP protocol but does not appear to use the term any longer; simply referring to it as the "RMI transport protocol". JRMP basically serves the same function as IIOP, but also supports object passing.

   Score: _____

   Notes: _____

5. What is a deployment descriptor?

   Skill Level: Low

   Expected answer:

   A deployment descriptor is an XML file that accompanies each module of a J2EE application. It describes the specific configuration requirements that need to be resolved for the module or application to be installed successfully to an application server.

   Score: _____

   Notes: _____

   _____

6. J2EE Enterprise Applications, with all of their modules (Web, client, business tier), are packaged into what type of file?

   Skill Level: Low

   Expected answer:

   They are packaged into an Enterprise Archive (EAR) file. An EAR file is nothing more than a standard Java Archive (JAR) file with an .ear extension.

   Score: _____

   Notes: _____

   _____

7. What types of files and modules can be found in an Enterprise Archive (EAR) file?

   Skill Level: Low

Expected answer:

An EAR file can comprise WAR, EJB JAR, RAR, and JAR files along with the application descriptor file; application.xml.

Score: _____

Notes: _____

_____

8. What are Web archive (WAR) files? What is the standard file extension to a WAR file?

   Skill Level: Low

   Expected answer:

   A WAR file is used to package *Java modules* for the purpose of deploying them to an application server. A WAR file has a standard file extension .war. A Web Archive (WAR) file is a Java archive file (created using the jar utility) used to store one or more of the following:

   - Descriptive meta-information
   - Java Servlets
   - JavaServer Pages (JSP)
   - Utility libraries and classes
   - Static documents, such as HTML files, images, and possibly sound files.
   - Client-side programs like applets, beans, and classes.

   A Web module can represent a stand-alone Web application, or it can be combined with other modules (for example, EJB modules) to form a full J2EE application.

Score: _____

Notes: _____

_____

9. What are the two transport protocols used by J2EE Web-based client applications?

   Skill Level: Low

   Expected answer:

   Web clients can use either the HTTP or HTTPS transport protocol.

   Score: _____

   Notes: _____

   _____

10. What is the Enterprise Information System (EIS) Tier within the J2EE environment?

    Skill Level: Medium

    Expected answer:

    The EIS tier includes your backend and legacy systems and normally includes the companies' Enterprise Resource Planning (ERP) system, mainframe transaction processing systems, database systems, and other legacy information systems. A typical J2EE enterprise application will need to communicate request and response processing with these legacy systems within the EIS Tier. Integrating new J2EE application with the EIS tier has assumed great importance because enterprises are striving to leverage their existing systems and resources while adopting and developing new technologies and architectures.

Score: _____

Notes: _____

11. What is the standard architecture used for connecting to the Enterprise Information System (EIS) tier from the J2EE platform?

    Skill Level: High

    Expected answer:

    The J2EE Connector Architecture.

    Score: _____

    Notes: _____

12. What are some of the types of containers defined in the J2EE architecture and what are they used for? Where are they located (client, application server, database server)?

    Skill Level: Low

    Expected answer:

    - **Application client container** - This type of container is found on the client machine and is responsible for running and managing the execution of all application client components for a single J2EE application. An applet container, for example, is a combination of a Web browser and Java plug-in located on the client machine.

    - **EJB container** - The EJB container is responsible for running and managing the execution of all enterprise beans for a single J2EE application. The EJB container is run on the application server.

- **Web container** - A Web container is responsible for running and managing the execution of all JSP and servlet components for a single J2EE application. The Web container and its components are run on the application server.

Score: _____

Notes: _____

_____

13. Why would you use a modeling tool for designing a J2EE application?

    Skill Level: Low

    Expected answer:

    Modeling tools are used to because of the increasing complexity of today's enterprise application systems and their components. These tools allow you to visualize the processes used for constructing and documenting the design and structure of an application. They also provide a means for showing the many components, their interdependencies, and how they relate to other components and subsystems in a large and complex application.

    Score: _____

    Notes: _____

    _____

14. What is the most popular modeling tool used for designing large and complex J2EE applications?

   Skill Level: Low

   Expected answer:

   The Unified Modeling Language (UML).

   Score: _____
   Notes: _____
   _____

15. What is a transaction?

   Skill Level: Medium

   Expected answer:

   A transaction is a bracket of processing or a sequence of information exchange and related work that represents a logical unit of work. It can be thought of as an "all or nothing" contract; all of the processing must be completed or else the transaction management component (sometimes called a transaction monitor) should restore (rollback) the application to the status as it was before the start of the transaction.

   Score: _____
   Notes: _____
   _____

16. What is ACID as it relates to transactions?

   Skill Level: High

Expected answer:

ACID is an acronym used to describe the four primary attributes ensured to any transaction by a transaction manager (sometimes called a transaction monitor or TP monitor). These attributes are:

- **Atomicity**. In a transaction involving two or more discrete pieces of information, either all of the pieces are committed or none are. This is sometimes referred to as the "all-or-nothing" property. This property defines that the entire sequence of operations are successful or the entire sequence is entirely unsuccessful. Successfully completed transactions are committed, while unsuccessful (partially executed) transactions are rolled back.

- **Consistency**. Transaction must always work on a consistent view of data. Also, when a transaction ends, it must leave the data in a consistent state. This property ensures that a transaction never leaves the database in a half-finished state. While a transaction is executing, it may be possible for certain constraints be violated (as with deferred transactions), but no other transaction will be allowed to see these inconsistencies. When the transaction ends, all such inconsistencies will have been eliminated.

- **Isolation**. For a given transaction that is in process and not yet committed, it must remain isolated from any other transaction. This property keeps transactions separated from each other until they're finished. For a given transaction, it should appear as though it is running all by itself – the effects of other concurrently running transactions on the system are invisible to this transaction. The effects of this transaction are invisible to others until the transaction is committed.

- **Durability**. This property defines that the results of any committed data is permanent. Committed data is saved by the system such that, even in the event of a failure and system restart, the data is available in its correct state.

  Score: _____
  Notes: _____
  _____

17. Are JAR files meant to be platform independent?

    Skill Level: Low

    Expected answer:

    Yes. JAR files are based on the popular ZIP file format and are cross-platform so developers do not have to worry about platform issues.

    Score: _____
    Notes: _____
    _____

18. What is the protocol used for communicating between CORBA object request brokers (ORBs)?

    Skill Level: Medium

    Expected answer:

    Internet Inter-ORB Protocol (IIOP)

    Score: _____
    Notes: _____
    _____

J2EE Development Concepts

19. What is Remote Method Invocation (RMI)?

    Skill Level: Low

    Expected answer:

    RMI is a distributed object model that allows a Java object running in one Java Virtual Machine (JVM) to invoke methods on another Java object running in a different JVM.

    Score: _____

    Notes: _____

    _____

20. You are designing a J2EE application that needs to implement asynchronous messaging? Which J2EE service would you use?

    Skill Level: Low

    Expected answer:

    Java Message Service (JMS).

    Score: _____

    Notes: _____

    _____

21. Which J2EE service API would you use to allow applications and J2EE servers to use transactions?

    Skill Level: Low

    Expected answer:

    Java Transaction API (JTA).

Score: _____

Notes: _____
_____
_____

Section average score: _____

Skill Level: _____

Java Server Pages (JSP)

1. JSP are not directly handled by the application container. What are JSPs converted to so they can be handled by the Web application container?

   Skill Level: Low

   Expected answer:

   JSPs are converted to servlets.

   Score: _____
   Notes: _____
   _____

2. Are you supposed to put JSP files in the same directory where Java servlets are stored?

   Skill Level: Low

   Expected answer:

   No. JSP files along with any other static pages (i.e. HTML files) that are to be called directly should be put in the application root directory for the application.

   Score: _____
   Notes: _____
   _____

3. Briefly describe the lifecycle of a JSP?

   Skill Level: Medium

Expected answer:

- **Translate the page.** All tags are converted to Java source code – a servlet.
- **Compile the page.** The Java source code (servlet) is compiled into a class file.
- **Load the class.** The servlet class gets loaded on its first request from a user.
- **Create an instance of the class.** The servlet container creates an instance of the class.
- **Make call to jspinit.** The servlet container will initialize the servlet instance by calling its jspinit method.
- **Make a call to _jspService.** The servlet container will then make a call to the _jspService method while passing in a *request* and *response* object.
- **Make a call to jspDestroy.** When the container needs to remove the JSP page from service, it will call the jspDestroy method.

Score: _____
Notes: _____
_____
_____

4. Why is the response to a JSP file always slow for the first client request?

   Skill Level: Medium

   Expected answer:

   When the JSP page is first called, it must go through a *translate* and *compile* stage which can be resource intensive. After it is converted to a servlet, the loads are very quick.

J2EE Development Concepts — **217**

Score: _____

Notes: _____

_____

5. Within a JSP page, you need to declare and initialize a String object named *database* to the value of "*Oracle*". How would you accomplish this?

   Skill Level: Low

   Expected answer:
   ```
   <%! String database = new String ("Oracle"); %>
   ```

   Score: _____

   Notes: _____

   _____

6. What are the two types of comments that can be put into a JSP page?

   Skill Level: Low

   Expected answer:
   ```
   HTML comment: <!-- comment -->
   JSP comment:  <%-- comment --%>
   ```

   Score: _____

   Notes: _____

   _____

7. Within a JSP page, you have access to several objects that are implicitly declared. One of those objects is the response object. What are some of the things you can do with this object?

Skill Level: High

Expected answer:

You can use the response object to perform the following:
- Add cookies
- Return an error page
- Add a header
- Redirect the browser to another URL
- Set the HTTP status

Score: _____

Notes: _____

8. How do you *import* other Java class files into your JSP page, just as you would do in a normal Java program?

Skill Level: Low

Expected answer:

You would use the import directive as shown in the following example:

```
<%@ page import="java.util.*;java.sql.*" %>
```

Score: _____

Notes: _____

9. If you have a JSP page that must retain the session of each client, what directive would you set to inform the translation step to instantiate an HttpSession object?

Skill Level: Medium

Expected answer:

At the page level, you would set the session attribute to *true* as shown in the following example:

```
<%@ page session="true" %>
```

Score: _____

Notes: _____

_____

10. What is the default value for the session attribute in a JSP page?

    Skill Level: Low

    Expected answer:

    True. If you do not session tracking, you would have to set the session attribute to false:

```
<%@ page session="false" %>
```

Score: _____

Notes: _____

_____

11. In a JSP file, how do you include the contents (source code) of another JSP into your code?

    Skill Level: Low

    Expected answer:

    You would use the include directive as shown in the following example:

```
<%@ include file="myOtherJspFile" %>
```

Score: _____

Notes: _____

_____

12. You have a JavaBean named "com.acme.myBean" that you would like to declare and use in a JSP file. The bean should be scoped for the *page* and the object to be named "myBean". What is the syntax to perform this?

    Skill Level: Low

    Expected answer:

    ```
    <jsp:useBean
        id="myBean"
        scope="page"
        class="com.acme.myBean"
    />
    ```

    Score: _____

    Notes: _____

    _____

13. You are using a JavaBean within a JSP and want this same bean object to be shared by different users. What would you set the scope attribute to when declaring the bean in order to allow this?

    Skill Level: Medium

    Expected answer:

    You would need to specify the scope attribute as "application" as shown in the following example:

    ```
    <jsp:useBean
        id="myBean"
        scope="application"
    ```

    J2EE Development Concepts   **221**

```
        class="com.acme.myBean"
/>
```

Score: _____

Notes: _____

_____

14. You have a JavaBean declared in your JSP page that is named with the ID = "myBean". How would you retrieve the attribute named "amount" from this object given a correctly defined JavaBean?

    Skill Level: Low

    Expected answer:

    Use the following syntax:

    ```
    <jsp:getProperty
        name="myBean"
        property="amount"
    />
    ```

    Score: _____

    Notes: _____

    _____

15. Which file contains the instructions to the container on where to find tab libraries by mapping a custom tag library URI to the actual tag library file?

    Skill Level: Medium

    Expected answer:

    The Web deployment descriptor file: Web.xml.

Score:

Notes:

16. You want to include a custom tag library in a JSP page. The URI for the library is "/myDBTagLibrary" and the tag prefix you want to use in your JSP page is "db". How would you write the tag library directive in your JSP page to perform this?

    Skill Level: Intermedaite

    Expected answer:

    ```
    <%@ taglib
        uri="/myDBTagLibrary"
        prefix="db"
    %>
    ```

    Score:

    Notes:

17. When writing a tag handler Java class, which class do you need to extend?

    Skill Level: High

    Expected answer:

    javax.servlet.jsp.tagext.TagSupport

    Score:

    Notes:

18. You have just coded and compiled a tag handler Java class to service custom tags in your JSP. Where do you put the tag handler classes?

    Skill Level: Medium

    Expected answer:

    The tag handler Java classes should be places in the WEB-INF/classes directory of your Web application.

    Score: _____
    Notes: _____
    _____
    _____

19. You have a JSP page that is not thread safe. What directive would you set to indicate this in your JSP page?

    Skill Level: Medium

    Expected answer:

    You would set the isThreadSafe attribute to false as shown in the following example:

    ```
    <%@ page isThreadSafe="false" %>
    ```

    Score: _____
    Notes: _____
    _____
    _____

20. How do you declare in a JSP page that it should use an error page named "appError.jsp"?

    Skill Level: Medium

Expected answer:

You would use the following:

```
<%@ page errorPage="appError.jsp" %>
```

Score: _____

Notes: _____
_____

Section average score: _____

Skill Level: _____

Java Beans

1. What is a JavaBean?

   Skill Level: Low

   Expected answer:

   A JavaBean is specification developed by Sun Microsystems that defines how Java objects interact. Specifically, they are reusable software components written in the Java programming language, designed to be manipulated visually by a software development environment (IDE), like JBuilder, Visual Age for Java, or JDeveloper – basically any application that understands the JavaBeans format.. JavaBeans are very similar to Microsoft's ActiveX components, but designed to be platform-neutral; running anywhere there is a Java Virtual Machine (JVM). JavaBeans can be dropped into an application container, (i.e. a form), and can then be used to perform functions ranging from a simple animation to complex calculations.

   Score: _____
   Notes: _____
   _____

2. How do JavaBeans differ from Enterprise JavaBeans?

   Skill Level: Medium

   Expected answer:

   The JavaBeans architecture is meant to provide a format for general-purpose components within a Java application. They are basically used to *"customize existing objects"*. Think about a button on a form that, when pressed, does not remain pressed – it bounces back to its off state, like a door-bell. The button acts as a single-state switch. Now you have to create a button that should have two stable states – like a typical light switch. In this case, you can take the existing button (the one having only one stable state) and "customize" it so that it has two stable states.

The Enterprise Java Beans (EJB) architecture, on the other hand, provides a format for highly specialized business (distributed) logic components. It is a completely distinctive concept than the one just mentioned above. EJB's are not used to customize an existing object. Instead they are used to "standardize" the way, in which business logic is written. For example, it is possible to write our business logic within the GUI logic, and also inside Servlets, Applets, and Standalone applications. Unfortunately, there is no clear distinction between the code that is responsible for the GUI and the actual business logic code, because all of the code is written inside the same class files. There is no chance for code reuse. By using EJBs, we can "componentize" the application by writing the business logic into separate class files than the GUI logic. This makes a clear distinction between the responsibilities of the GUI logic and the business logic.

Score: _____

Notes: _____

_____

3. What type of constructor is required for a class to be considered a JavaBean?

Skill Level: Low

Expected answer:

It must have a "no-arg" constructor.

Score: _____

Notes: _____

_____

4. What are the four requirements of a Java class to be considered a JavaBean?

   Skill Level: Medium

   Expected answer:

   - The class must contain a no-arg constructor.
   - The class will use standardized method names (getter/setter method naming paradigm) for property assessors and mutators.
   - There are no public instance variables.
   - The class must be public.

   Score: _____

   Notes: _____

   _____

5. You want to include a JavaBean in a JSP page. Which three attributes should be supplied?

   Skill Level: Medium

   Expected answer:

   - An ID – which provides a local name for the bean

- The Bean's Class Name – which is used to instantiate the bean if it does not exit
- A Scope – which specifies the lifetime of the bean, which by default is "page"

Score: _____

Notes: _____

6. What would the syntax be if you wanted to include a JavaBean in a JSP with the following attributes:

ID   = "myBean"
Class = "com.acme.MyBean"
Scope = "session"

Skill Level: Low

Expected answer:

```
<jsp:useBean
     id="myBean"
     class="com.mycompany.MyBean"
     scope="session"
/>
```

Score: _____

Notes: _____

7. What are the possible values for the "scope" attribute when initiating a JavaBean within a JSP document using the jsp:useBean action? What is the default value?

Skill Level: Medium

J2EE Development Concepts

Expected answer:

The scope attribute defines the scope within which the reference is available. The possible values are *page*, *request*, *session*, and *application*. The default for the scope attribute is *page*.

Score:
Notes:

8. You are using a JavaBean in a JSP and want to provide initial values when the bean gets created. How do you perform this?

   Skill Level: High

   Expected answer:

   You would put the initialization code in the body of the jsp:useBean action tag. The body will not be executed if the bean already exists. Here is an example that utilizes the values used in the previous question:

   ```
   <jsp:useBean id="myBean"
             class="com.mycompany.MyBean"
             scope="session">
     <%-- this body is executed only if the
          bean is created. Now let's
          initialize some of the bean
          properties. --%>
     <jsp:setProperty name="myBean"
                   property="prop1"
                   value="123" />
   </jsp:useBean>
   ```

   Score:
   Notes:

9. You have included and initiated a JavaBean in a JSP named "myBean". What is the syntax of the action to perform in order to print the value of the property "prop1" to the generated output?

   Skill Level: Low

   Expected answer:

   ```
   <jsp:getProperty   name="myBean"
                      property="prop1">
   ```

   Score: _____

   Notes: _____
   _____

10. When you include a JavaBean in a JSP using the jsp:useBean action, it declares a local Java variable to hold the bean object. What is the local Java variable name that it creates?

    Skill Level: Medium

    Expected answer:

    The name of the local Java variable that gets created from the jsp:useBean action is exactly the value of the ID attribute. In the action below, a local Java variable named "useBean" will be created.

    ```
    <jsp:useBean
         id="myBean"
         class="com.mycompany.MyBean"
         scope="session"
    />
    ```

    Score: _____

    Notes: _____
    _____

J2EE Development Concepts

Section average score: _____

Skill Level: _____

C Programming Questions

1. Explain the use of the compiler directive `#include` ?

   Skill Level: Low

   Expected answer:

   `#include` instructs the compiler to insert the contents of a file.

   Score: _____

   Notes: _____

   _____

2. Explain the use of the compiler directive `#define` ?

   Skill Level: Low

   Expected answer:

   It is used to set known values for the compiler. You can use it to state a known value's name for example: `#define DEBUG` or to state a substituted value for example: `#define NEWVALUE 8`.

   Score: _____

   Notes: _____

   _____

3. Explain the use of the compiler directive `#pragma` ?

   Skill Level: Medium

   Expected answer:

   `#pragma` alerts the compiler that the following instructions are to be ignored if the compiler does not understand them.

Score: _____

Notes: _____

_____

4. What directive is used to designate the end of a `#if` block of code?

   Skill Level: Low

   Expected answer:

   `#endif`

   Score: _____

   Notes: _____

   _____

5. What markers are used to define comments within C code?

   Skill Level: Low

   Expected answer:

   /* and */

   Score: _____

   Notes: _____

   _____

6. What symbols can be used in an identifier?

   Skill Level: Low

   Expected answer:

   Only the underscore can be used in the name of an identifier.

Score: _____

Notes: _____

_____

7. What symbol goes at the end of each C statement?

   Skill Level: Low

   Expected answer:

   A semicolon goes at the end of each C statement.

   Score: _____

   Notes: _____

   _____

8. Describe a block.

   Skill Level: Low

   Expected answer:

   A block is a series of C statements which are contained within a pair of curly braces.

   Score: _____

   Notes: _____

   _____

9. Can a C structure include a pointer to itself?

   Skill Level: Low

   Expected answer:

   Yes

Score: _____

Notes: _____

_____

10. Is void main() the correct declaration for main()?

    Skill Level: Low

    Expected answer:

    No

    Score: _____

    Notes: _____

    _____

11. What is the name of the function that every C program must contain and is the starting point for execution of your C program? How many times must it appear?

    Skill level: Medium

    Expected answer:

    main() .

    It can appear only once.

    Score: _____

    Notes: _____

    _____

12. What are the three techniques to define a constant variable in C?

    Skill Level: High

Expected answer:

Using the preprocessor directive `#define`:

For example:
```
#define pi 3.1415
```

Using the `const` keyword when defining the variable:

For example:
```
const float pi = 3.1415;
```

The third technique is to use an enumeration. An enumeration is used to define a set of constants. This is a useful technique to define a set of constants as opposed to using multiple #define preprocessor directives.

For example:

```
enum days {
    Monday=1
    , Tuesday
    , Wednesday
    , Thursday
    , Friday
    , Saturday
    , Sunday
};
```

Score: _____

Notes: _____

_____

13. What is a function prototype?

   Skill level: Medium

C Programming Questions   **237**

Expected answer:

> A function prototype is used to declare a function before it is actually used. It is considered good programming practice to declare all functions before their use. A function prototype declares the function name, its parameters, and its return type to the rest of the program prior to the function's actual declaration.

Score: _____

Notes: _____

_____

14. What is the name of the C library that contains standard I/O functions and how would you include it in a C program?

    Skill level: Medium

    Expected answer:

    > The name of the C library that contains standard I/O functions is **stdio.h**. Here is an example of how to include this in a C program:

    ```
    ...
    #include <stdio.h>
    ...
    ```

    Score: _____

    Notes: _____

    _____

15. Consider the code segment below. Why does this code print out that the values are equal? What would you do to correct this program?

    ```
    1:   #include <stdio.h>
    2:
    ```

238   Conducting the Web Designer Job Interview

```
 3:  main() {
 4:
 5:     int a=5;
 6:     int b=8;
 7:
 8:     if (a=b) {
 9:        printf("The two values are equal.\n");
10:     } else {
11:        printf("The two values are NOT equal.\n");
12:     }
13:
14: }

% a.out
The two values are equal.
```

Skill level: Low

Expected answer:

> The C programming language uses the == operator for checking equality. In our example, we accidentally used the = operator in line 8, which is used to assign a value. To correct the program, we would replace line 8 with the following

```
8: if (a == b) {
```

Score: _____

Notes: _____

_____

16. Write a simple code segment that declares a five element integer array named "a". After creating the array, continue the code segment by assigning an integer value to each of the 5 elements in the array. Finish off the example by looping through the array and printing each element to STDOUT using a FOR loop.

Skill level: Medium

Expected answer:

Here is an example code segment:

```
#include <stdio.h>

main() {
   int a[5];
   int i;

   a[0] = 10;
   a[1] = 20;
   a[2] = 30;
   a[3] = 40;
   a[4] = 50;

   for (i=0; i<5; i++) {
      printf("Element [%d] = %d\n", i, a[i]);
   }

}

% a.out
Element [0] = 10
Element [1] = 20
Element [2] = 30
Element [3] = 40
Element [4] = 50
```

Score: _____

Notes: _____

_____

17. What type of variable in C is used to store a memory address that can be used to point to another variable?

    Skill level: Medium

    Expected answer:

    A *pointer* variable.

Score: _____

Notes: _____

_____

18. Write a sample code segment that declares two variables: (1) A normal integer variable named **i** that is assigned the value of 5 and (2) A pointer to an integer variable named **j**. After declaring the two variables, assign the memory address of the variable **i** to **j**. Finally, print the value being pointed to by the variable **j** to standard out.

    Skill level: High

    Expected answer:

Score: _____

Notes: _____

_____

19. Is there a problem with the code segment below? If so, how would you fix it?

    ```
    #include <stdio.h>

    main() {

       int i=5;
       int *j;

       j = &i;

       printf("The value pointed to by j is %d.\n", *j);

    }

    % a.out
    The value pointed to by j is 5.
    ```

    Skill level: High

C Programming Questions

Expected answer:

The code segment above contains a common bug and will often cause a *segmentation fault* (core dump) when run. This is caused by attempting to use an un-initialized pointer variable. To fix this program, we should initialize the pointer variable p as in the following code:

```
#include <stdio.h>

main() {

   int *p;
   p = (int *) malloc(1*sizeof(int));   /* Initialize Pointer */
   *p = 5;

   printf("The value pointed to by p is %d.\n", *p);

}
```

Score: _____

Notes: _____

_____

20. Why is it important to check the return value from a call to the *malloc()* function?

Skill level: Medium

Expected answer:

You should always check the return value of any call to the *malloc()* function as the return value can be used to determine if *malloc()* was actually able to allocate the requested memory from the heap. If the *malloc()* function returns a value of zero, this indicates that the *malloc()* function was not able to allocate the requested amount of memory - more than likely because the machine is out of memory.

Score: _____
Notes: _____
_____

21. Explain how Typedef names are automatically created for structure tags?

    Skill Level: Medium

    Expected answer:

    They aren't automatically created.

    Score: _____
    Notes: _____
    _____

22. What would you be doing to a file if you used the function *mmap()* and then used the function *sizeof()*?

    Skill level: Medium

    Expected answer:

    Attempting to learn the size of the file before reading it in.

    Score: _____
    Notes: _____
    _____

Section average score: _____

Skill Level: _____

C Programming Questions

C ++ Questions

1. Explain why you might need to use Language-Adaptable Header Files in a C++ program.

   Skill Level: Low

   Expected answer:

   C++ programs will often need to interface with C programs so it is important for the header file to be compatible with the C standards.

   Score: _____
   Notes: _____
   _____

2. Explain the significance of using Idempotent Header Files?

   Skill Level: Low

   Expected answer:

   An idempotent header file is one that works with multiple inclusions. An effective header file needs to be capable of adapting to different versions of C and C++.

   Score: _____
   Notes: _____
   _____

3. Which kind of comment automatically ends at the end of a line?

   Skill Level: Low

Expected answer:

> A comment that is marked with a double slash (//) terminates at the end of a line.

Score: _____

Notes: _____

_____

4. Explain what is required to end a comment that originates with a slash and a star (/*)?

   Skill Level: Low

   Expected answer:

   > A slash star comment will continue from line to line unless you insert a star slash (*/) to signal the end of the comment.

   Score: _____

   Notes: _____

   _____

5. Is C++ case sensitive?

   Skill Level: Low

   Expected answer:

   > Yes

   Score: _____

   Notes: _____

   _____

6. Explain the significance of white space in C++ statements?

   Skill Level: Low

   Expected answer:

   Whitespace within statements is usually ignored. However, it can be used to make statements easier to read.

   Score: _____

   Notes: _____

   _____

7. What is an expression?

   Skill Level: Low

   Expected answer:

   In C++ an expression is a statement that returns a value. For example 4+5; provides the value 9 making it an expression.

   Score: _____

   Notes: _____

   _____

8. Explain why constants are always l-values?

   Skill Level: Low

   Expected answer:

   They aren't! Constants are r-values which means they reside on the right side of an assignment operator.

Score: _____

Notes: _____

_____

9. What is an assignment operator?

    Skill Level: Low

    Expected answer:

    The equal sign (=) is an assignment operator which causes the operand on the left side to have its value changed to the value that is displayed on the right side.

    Score: _____

    Notes: _____

    _____

10. Explain why constants are always r-values?

    Skill Level: Low

    Expected answer:

    Constants are considered r-values because they reside on the right side of an assignment operator.

    Score: _____

    Notes: _____

    _____

11. Explain the modulus operator?

    Skill Level: Medium

Expected answer:

> The modulus operator is the mathematical operator that is used to determine the remainder that is dropped after an integer division.

Score: _____

Notes: _____

_____

12. Why do you always include a semicolon after an *if* statement?

    Skill Level: Low

    Expected answer:

    > You should never include a semicolon after an *if* statement as it will terminate the statement causing it to be ineffective.

    Score: _____

    Notes: _____

    _____

13. Explain the result of the expression income += 1000?

    Skill Level: Low

    Expected answer:

    > The result would be the value of income plus 1000 so assuming income equals 50,000 the result would be 51,000.

    Score: _____

    Notes: _____

    _____

14. What is the increment operator? What does it do?

   Skill Level: Low

   Expected answer:

   The increment operator is plus plus (++) and it increases a variable's value by one.

   Score: _____

   Notes: _____

   _____

15. What is the decrement operator? What does it do?

   Skill Level: Low

   Expected answer:

   The decrement operator is minus minus (--) and it decreases a variable's value by one.

   Score: _____

   Notes: _____

   _____

16. Explain the two varieties of the increment and decrement operators? What do they do?

   Skill Level: Low

   Expected answer:

   - When the operator is placed before the variable name it falls in the prefix category and when it comes after the variable name it is of the postfix variety.

- When the operator is in the prefix position it is processed before the assignment, when in the postfix position it is processed after assignment.

Score: _____

Notes: _____

17. What is the result of the following statement?

    ```
    a = 7 + 2 * 6;
    ```

    Skill Level: Low

    Expected answer:

    The answer would be 19 because the multiplication operation is performed before the addition.

    Score: _____

    Notes: _____

18. In what order are nested parentheses read?

    Skill Level: Medium

    Expected answer:

    Nested parentheses are read from the inside out.

    Score: _____

    Notes: _____

19. Can you name six relational operators?

   Skill Level: Low

   Expected answer:

   The six relational operators are equals (==), not equals (!=), greater than (>), less than (<), greater than or equal to (>=) and less than or equal to (<=).

   Score: _____

   Notes: _____

   _____

20. Can you name three logical operators?

   Skill Level: Low

   Expected answer:

   The three logical operators are:
   - And   &&
   - Or ||
   - Not   !

   Score: _____

   Notes: _____

   _____

21. What is a C++ ternary operator? Explain what it does.

   Skill Level: Medium

C ++ Questions

Expected answer:

> The ternary operator (?:) is a conditional operator which processes three expressions and returns the appropriate value.

Score: _____

Notes: _____

_____

22. What is the difference between direct and indirect recursion?

    Skill Level: Medium

    Expected answer:

    > Direct recursion is a function calling itself. It is indirect recursion when a function calls another function which in turn calls the first function.

    Score: _____

    Notes: _____

    _____

23. What are C++ classes?

    Skill Level: Medium

    Expected answer:

    > Classes are data types that you create including data members or variables of various types which are called objects. Classes also contain methods or member functions which are used to perform services and manipulate the member data.

Score: _____

Notes: _____

_____

24. What is a virtual copy constructor?

Skill Level: Medium

Expected answer:

A virtual copy constructor is a copy constructor which has been called by a virtual method within a class.

Score: _____

Notes: _____

_____

Section average score: _____

Skill Level: _____

Non-Technical Questions

When conducting an on-site or telephone interview, it's very important that you be able to assess non-technical information about your job candidate. These non-technical factors include motivation, thinking skills, and personal attitude. All of these factors have a direct bearing on the ultimate success of the candidate in your shop. They also give you an idea about the potential longevity of a particular candidate.

Each of these questions is deliberately ambiguous and probing so that the job candidate will have an opportunity to speak freely. Often these questions will give you a very good idea of the suitability of the candidate for the position. Remember, in many IT shops technical ability is secondary to the ability of the candidate to function as a team member within the organization.

1. What are your plans if you don't get this job?

    Answer: _____

    Comment: _____

    _____

This question can reveal a great deal about the motivation of the job candidate. If the candidate indicates that he/she will change career fields, going into an unrelated position, then this person may not have a long-term motivation to stay within the IT industry. If, on the other hand, the candidate responds that he will continue to pursue opportunities within the specific technical area, then the candidate is probably dedicated to the job for which he is being interviewed.

2. How do you feel about overtime?

    Answer: _____

    Comment: _____

    _____

This is an especially loaded question, because any honest job candidate is going to tell you that they don't like to work overtime. As we know, the reality of today's IT world is that the professional will occasionally have to work evenings and weekends. This question is essential if you're interviewing for a position that requires non-traditional hours, such as a network administrator or database administrator, where the bulk of the production changes will occur on evenings, weekends, and holidays.

3. Describe your biggest non-technical flaw.

    Answer: _____

    Comment: _____

    _____

This question provides insight into the personality of the job candidate, as well as their honesty and candor. Responses are unpredictable and may range from "I don't suffer fools gladly" to "I have difficulty thinking after I've been on the job for 16 hours". Again, there is no right or wrong answer to this question, but it may indicate how well the candidate is going to function during critical moments. More importantly, this question gives an idea of the level of self-awareness of the candidate and gauges whether or not they are actively working to improve their non-technical skills.

4. Describe your least favorite boss or professor.

    Answer: _____
    Comment: _____
    _____

   The answer to this question will reveal the candidate's opinions and attitudes about being supervised by others. While there is no correct response to this question, it can shed a great deal of light on the candidate's interpersonal skills.

5. Where do you plan to be ten years from now?

    Answer: _____
    Comment: _____
    _____

   This is an especially important question for the IT job candidate because it reveals a lot about their motivations. As we know, the IT job industry does not have a lot of room for advancement within the technical arena, and someone who plans to rise within the IT organization will be required to move into management at some point. It's interesting that the response to this question is often made to be overly important, especially amongst those managers that hear the response "in ten years I would like to have your job."

6. How important is money to you?

      Answer: _____

      Comment: _____

      _____

Again, this is an extremely misleading question, because even though many IT professionals deeply enjoy their jobs, and some would even do it for free, money is a primary motivator for people in the workplace. This question provides an easy opportunity to find out whether or not your candidate is being honest with you.

An appropriate answer for the candidate might be to say that he greatly enjoys his work within IT but that he needs to be able to maintain some level of income in order to support his family. A bonus benefit of this question is it also provides insight into the demographic structure of the job candidate, namely their marital status, as well as the age of their children, and whether or not they have immediate family in the area. It is well known within the IT industry that job candidates are most likely to remain with the company if they have a large extended family group within the immediate area

7. Why did you leave your last job?

      Answer: _____

      Comment: _____

      _____

This is one of the most loaded questions of all, and one that can be extremely revealing about the personality of the

IT job candidate. The most appropriate answer to this question is that the previous job was not technically challenging enough, or that the candidate was bored.

However, periodically you will find job candidates who will express negativity regarding the work environment, the quality of the management, and the personalities of the co-workers. This of course, should be a major red flag because it may indicate that this job candidate does not possess the interpersonal skills required to succeed in a team environment.

8. If you were a vegetable, what vegetable would you be?

    Answer: _____
    Comment: _____
    _____

On its face, this is a totally ludicrous and ambiguous question, but it gives you an opportunity to assess the creative thinking skills of the job candidate. For example, if the job candidate merely replies "I don't know", he may not possess the necessary creative thinking skills required for a systems analyst or developer position.

A creative candidate will simply pick a vegetable, and describe in detail why that particular vegetable suits their personality. For example, the job candidate might say "I would be broccoli because I am health-oriented, have a bushy head, and go well with Chinese food."

9. Describe the month of June.

    Answer: _____

    Comment: _____

    _____

The answer to this question also provides insight into the thinking ability of the job candidate. For example, most job candidates may reply that June is a summer month, with longer days, hot weather, and an ideal vacation time. The candidate with an engineering or scientific point of view might reply instead that June is a month with 30 days that immediately precedes the summer equinox.

10. Why do you want to work here?

    Answer: _____

    Comment: _____

    _____

This is the candidate's opportunity to express why he might be a good fit for your particular organization. It also indicates whether the candidate has taken the time to research the company and the work environment. Is the candidate applying for this position solely because he needs a job, any job, or because he has specifically singled out your company due to some appealing characteristic of the work environment?

This question can also add information about the motivation of the job candidate, because a job candidate who is highly motivated to work for a particular firm will make the effort to research the company, the work environment, and even the backgrounds of individual managers.

Using a powerful search engine such as Google, the savvy IT candidate can quickly glean information about the person who is interviewing them. Having detailed knowledge of the organization is a very positive indicator that the candidate has given a lot of thought to the particular position and is evidence of high motivation.

11. What do you know about our company?

>   Answer: _____
>   Comment: _____
>   _____

If the prospective employee has little or no knowledge about the company, then he will also have little idea about how he can benefit the company. A candidate who has not gone to the trouble of researching the organization may be after a job, any job.

A candidate who has taken the time to explore the company will probably have specific ideas in mind about what he can bring to the organization. The initiative required by the candidate to research the company is a good sign that he is proactive and not passive dead weight.

If the candidate has some knowledge of the company's mission and function, this will also become apparent in the questions he asks you. He will already be thinking about how he can fit in and how his skills can be utilized. These are desirable traits of a problem-solver.

12. Why do you want to work for this company? Why should we hire you?

    Answer: _____

    Comment: _____

    _____

The answer to this question can reveal whether the candidate is merely shopping for a job or has true interest in the company and the position. It is important that the candidate show some passion for the field. If he does not, he will probably never be creative in the work environment and he will not represent a solution for you.

Does the candidate have a core belief that his particular set of skills can benefit you? Answers such as "I believe my experience can make a difference here," or "I believe your company will provide an environment that more directly engages my interest," or "Working for your company will provide challenges that excite me" are good starters.

13. Why are you looking for a new job?

    Answer: _____

    Comment: _____

    _____

Typical reasons for seeking a new job include the desire to advance in the field and boredom in a job that offers few fresh challenges. These are positive motivations, but there can be negative ones as well. There may be personal conflicts between the candidate and other team members or management that have become so adversarial that the candidate is compelled to leave.

While not necessarily eliminating a candidate from consideration, personal friction in the previous job does raise a red flag. It may be that the candidate is an unfortunate victim of backroom politics. However, if he confides in you regarding the shortcomings of his supervisors or fellow employees while taking no responsibility himself, consider yourself warned.

14. Tell us about yourself or your background.

>	Answer: _____
>	Comment: _____
>	_____

This is probably asked more than any other question in interviews. It is the main opportunity for the candidate to describe his experiences, motivations, and vision of himself as it relates to the company.

The candidate should provide clear examples of how his abilities were used in the past to solve problems. If the candidate just repeats the information in the résumé, he is probably only going through the motions and has no clear vision of his role in the company.

Even worse, if the candidate contradicts the résumé, there is evidence of a serious problem.

15. What are three major characteristics that you bring to the job?

    Answer: _____

    Comment: _____

    _____

The candidate should offer specific skills or traits that he believes will be useful in the position. If the candidate is unable to relate these characteristics to the job, he has obviously not thought much about his role in the organization. You are interested in finding someone who has ideas about how he can hit the ground running and make a real difference to the company.

16. Describe the "ideal" job... the "ideal" supervisor.

    Answer: _____

    Comment: _____

    _____

This question is not as open-ended as it may seem. If the candidate's ideal job has little or nothing in common with the position he is interviewing for, he is unlikely to be a good fit. The candidate's response should match fairly well with the requirements of the position.

The candidate's description of the ideal supervisor can provide clues about how well the candidate works with superiors. Beware the candidate who seizes this as an opportunity to denigrate past managers.

17. How would you handle a tough customer?

    Answer: _____

    Comment: _____

    _____

Can the candidate provide examples of instances when difficult clients were won over? An effective communicator can strike a balance between meeting the needs of the customer and dealing with unrealistic expectations.

Above all, the candidate should indicate that he understands the necessity of "going the extra mile" to alleviate the concerns of the customer. Providing service to the client or end user is fundamental to the success of any enterprise.

18. How would you handle working with a difficult co-worker?

    Answer: _____

    Comment: _____

    _____

This is similar to the last question. The candidate should relate an example of a conflict with a co-worker or team member that was successfully resolved. What you are looking for is evidence that the candidate is able to facilitate communication and lead a difficult project to a successful conclusion.

19. When would you be available to start if you were selected?

    Answer: _____

    Comment: _____

    _____

20. How does this position match your career goals?

    Answer: _____

    Comment: _____

    _____

This is an excellent question to ascertain whether the candidate truly sees the position as an integral part of his career path. Does the candidate believe the knowledge and experience he will gain from this job will move him to where he wants to be?

A thorough answer to this question will lead into the next one.

21. What are your career goals (a) 3 years from now; (b) 10 years from now?

    Answer: _____

    Comment: _____

    _____

The answer to this question will indicate the level of commitment the candidate feels towards the job and the company. If the candidate has a goal in mind, how well does it fit with the job he is applying for?

When the candidate describes his goals, does he speak in terms of the skills and abilities he hopes to acquire that will prepare him for his eventual role, or does he simply want to be the CEO, with little thought of what it might take to get there?

The interviewer may be surprised by how often the candidate will talk about goals that are unrelated to the position.

22. What do you like to do in your spare time?

Answer: _____
Comment: _____
_____

This question provides an opportunity to learn more about the character of the candidate, and to judge whether his outside interests complement his professional life. Is the candidate well-rounded or one-dimensional? Does he tend to sustain an interest over time?

23. What motivates you to do a good job?

Answer: _____
Comment: _____
_____

If the candidate responds "making money" or "avoiding the wrath of my boss," you may have a problem. The candidate should describe some positive motivation, such as a new challenge, and tie it to a specific example of a time in the past when the motivation reaped personal rewards and results on the job.

24. What two or three things are most important to you at work?

    Answer: _____

    Comment: _____

    _____

The answer to this can reveal much about how the candidate sees himself on the job. Does the candidate mention things such as the importance of interpersonal communication, or responding quickly to crisis situations, things that facilitate job performance, or does he seem to be more worried about the timeliness of his coffee breaks?

25. What qualities do you think are essential to be successful in this kind of work?

    Answer: _____

    Comment: _____

    _____

Does the candidate have a realistic idea of what the work environment requires of him, and do the qualities of the candidate match the job? Does the candidate have an example of a past job experience when these qualities were called upon with beneficial results?

26. How does your previous work experience prepare you for this position?

    Answer: _____

    Comment: _____

    _____

This question is related to many of the others. If the candidate is able to articulate a clear idea of how his previous experience and training has prepared him for the responsibilities of the new position, he will be well ahead of many other interviewees.

27. How do you define "success?"

    Answer: _____

    Comment: _____

    _____

If the answer doesn't fit the position, the candidate may be unhappy in the field or quickly become bored. This indicates that the candidate may not be committed to staying with the company for very long.

28. What has been your most significant accomplishment to date?

    Answer: _____

    Comment: _____

    _____

The candidate should be able to relate a specific example of an achievement that demonstrates a desirable quality for the job. The candidate should focus on action and results, rather than long-winded descriptions of situations.

The answer to this question can provide insight into situations that the candidate may handle especially well. The candidate should demonstrate an ability to persevere and overcome obstacles. Did the person deliver more than was expected of him in a difficult situation?

29. Describe a failure and how you dealt with it.

     Answer: _____

     Comment: _____

     _____

This type of negative question can be extremely revealing. It can indicate significant weaknesses or problems that may interfere with the ability to do the job.

Was the failure a catastrophic one, or a relatively minor problem? Was the candidate able to learn from the experience and apply the knowledge to future situations?

The answer to this question can also reveal how much personal accountability and responsibility the candidate accepts. If the candidate blames the failure on others, he is not likely to learn from his mistakes.

As with most interview questions, this questions is designed to provide insight into the overall personality of the candidate, giving you a fuller appreciation of the strengths, as well as the weaknesses, of the person.

30. What leadership roles have you held?

Answer: _____
Comment: _____
_____

This answer should indicate not only that the candidate has the leadership experience to succeed in the new job, but that he has the ability to work well with others and is able to shoulder the responsibility and deal with the pressure associated with the requirements of the position.

31. Are you willing to travel?

Answer: _____
Comment: _____
_____

The answer here will demonstrate how committed to the company the candidate is likely to be. If the candidate dismisses the idea of travel completely, he may lack the motivation you are looking for.

32. What have you done in the past year to improve yourself?

Answer: _____
Comment: _____
_____

This question can shed more light on the personality of the candidate. If the candidate has been motivated by the goal of obtaining this position, he will be able to demonstrate that he has taken the initiative to prepare himself for it.

If the candidate instead chooses to describe the benefits of his basket-weaving class, he may indeed be the better for it, but it has little relevance to solving the problems he would soon encounter in the new position.

33. In what areas do you feel you need further education and training to be successful?

Answer: _____
Comment: _____
_____

If the answer has nothing to do with the offered position, the candidate may soon become bored. This question is similar to others and should dovetail with other answers about goals and career path.

34. What are your salary requirements?

Answer: _____
Comment: _____
_____

If the candidate mentions a figure that is too low, he may be uninformed or desperate. On the other hand, if his financial expectations are unreasonable, he should probably be eliminated from consideration.

Policies, Processes and Procedures

The following questions are designed to zero in on key aspects of the candidate's personality and ability to perform. You may find it helpful to assign each response a score between 1 and 5 (a shorthand assessment technique that may also be used with many of the preceding questions).

You are trying to gauge the candidate's ability to act in accordance with established guidelines, follow standard procedures in crisis situations, communicate and enforce organizational policies and procedures, and recognize and constructively conform to unwritten rules or practices.

1. On some jobs it is necessary to act strictly in accordance with policy. Give me an example when you were expected to act in accordance with policy even when it was not convenient. What did you do?

    Expected answer: Did the candidate follow policy because of commitment to it, even if a reason could be given for breaking it? Was there non-conformity to policy because of personal style, disrespect for those who made the policy, or revenge/dishonesty?

    Score: _____
    Comment: _____
    _____

2. What types of experience have you had in managing situations that involve potentially high money loss situations to ensure your job effectiveness?

    Expected answer: Did the candidate have a "no exceptions" strategy which showed systematic and rigorous use of policy and procedures to ensure consistency? Was there a dislike for rules and preferences to ensure consistency? Was there dislike for rules and preference for doing the job his/her own way?

Score: _____

Comment: _____

_____

3. Describe a time when you found a policy or procedure challenging or difficult to adhere to. How did you handle it

   Expected answer: Did the candidate take great pains to adhere to the policy and communicate the difficulty to proper management for review/revision? Was there an unnecessary risky deviation from policy, and no communication of either the challenge or deviation to management?

   Score: _____

   Comment: _____

   _____

Quality

The traits of a candidate who does quality work include their ability to maintain high standards despite pressing deadlines, establish high standards and measures, do work right the first time, inspect material for flaws, test new methods thoroughly, and reinforce excellence as a fundamental priority.

1. Describe a situation in which a crucial deadline was nearing, but you didn't want to compromise quality. How did you deal with it?

    Expected answer: Did the candidate maintain high quality through investing additional resources, moving deadlines, or making a statement of work in progress? Was there a quality sacrifice, possibly resulting in additional problems at a later time?

    Score: _____

    Comment: _____
    _____

2. Describe something you developed or coordinated that had to be exactly right. Exactly how did you test it?

    Expected answer: Did the candidate rigorously identify potential sources of problems, systematically address them, and run ample trails? Was there a brief accounting for possible problems, insufficient experimentation, or minimal piloting?

    Score: _____

    Comment: _____
    _____

3. Describe an effort you undertook to make product/service quality a fundamental priority in your business. Exactly what steps did you take to do this?

   Expected answer: Did the candidate implement training and error prevention/control/correction systems, or apply other systematic approaches? Was there a haphazard or inadequate support of quality functions?

   Score: _____

   Comment: _____

   _____

Commitment to Task

Commitment to task involves the ability to take responsibility for actions and outcomes and persist despite obstacles. To be available around the clock in case of emergency, give long hours to the job, demonstrate dependability in difficult circumstances, and show a sense of urgency about getting the job done.

1. Describe a difficult situation in which you took full responsibility for actions and outcomes. How did you act on this?

    Expected answer: Did the candidate publicly claim responsibility, and then carefully manage this situation to success, possibly one involving other parties with divergent goals? Was there allowance of others to accept blame, and little effort to resolve a difficult situation?

    Score: _____

    Comment: _____

    _____

2. Some people can be counted on to go the extra mile when their organization really needs it. Describe a time when you demonstrated dependability in trying circumstances.

    Expected answer: Did the candidate work long hours or perform unusual job duties to help the organization get through a personnel shortage, etc.? Was there minimal extra effort, consistent with the notion that it was the company's problem?

    Score: _____

    Comment: _____

    _____

3. Describe a time when you gave long hours to the job. For example, tell me about when you took work home, worked on weekends, or maintained long hours due to system maintenance.

   Expected answer: Did the candidate show self-direction and initiative in working particularly long hours, with clear dedication to a meaningful objective? Was there compliance to routine work requirements, possibly with resentment about what was expected?

   Score: _____
   Comment: _____
   _____

4. Give me an example of a time when you demonstrated a sense of urgency about getting results.

   Expected answer: Did the candidate take immediate action directed toward a specific objective, so that non-task activities and interests were given low priority while productivity and efficiency were of prime importance? Was there little emphasis on effectiveness/speed/efficiency?

   Score: _____
   Comment: _____
   _____

Planning, Prioritizing and Goal Setting

Your network administrator may be called upon to wear many different hats in this position. He/She should have the ability to prepare for emerging customer needs, manage multiple projects, and determine project urgency in a meaningful and practical way. Other desirable abilities include the ability to use goals to guide actions and create detailed action plans and the ability to organize and schedule people and tasks.

1. Describe a situation that illustrates how well you manage multiple projects simultaneously.

    Expected answer: Did the candidate keep all projects moving on a pace to hit deadlines and in a manageable, systematic, quality way, and using a meaningful approach to prioritizing? Was there haphazard allotment of resources to different tasks, with unproductive and unnecessary chaos?

    Score: _____
    Comment: _____
    _____

2. Priorities can be set meaningfully based on ease of task, customer size, deadlines, or a number of other factors. Describe a time when it was challenging for you to prioritize.

    Expected answer: Did the candidate use a sensible set or priorities and apply it consistently? Was there excess bouncing of resources, resulting in inefficiency, or a poor choice of criteria on which to prioritize?

Score: _____

Comment: _____

_____

3. Think of a project in which you skillfully coordinated people, tasks, and schedules. How did you do it?

   Expected answer: Did the candidate use a systematic approach to identify tasks, people who can do the tasks, schedules, and constraints? Was there a simplistic approach that was inadequate given the complexities of the project?

   Score: _____

   Comment: _____

   _____

Attention to Detail

Attention to detail involves the ability to be alert in a high-risk environment, the ability to follow detailed procedures and ensure accuracy in documentation and data. Your network administrator may be called upon to carefully monitor gauges, instruments, or processes. He/She should be able to concentrate on routine work details and organize and maintain a system of records.

1. Describe a time when you had to apply changes to a mission critical system. What did you do to insure the stability of the system? What actions did you take and what were the results?

    Expected answer: Did the candidate dutifully monitor all potentially troublesome aspects of the environment, and address anything that seemed imperfect. Was there a casual awareness of potential trouble spots, and reliance on subsequent quick reactions rather than prevention?

    Score: _____
    Comment: _____
    _____

2. Select an experience from you past, which illustrates your ability to be attentive to detail when monitoring the systems environment. Tell me, in detail, what happened.

    Expected answer: Did the candidate show commitment to monitoring and understanding equipment and to using a strategy to ensure/enhance attention to detail? Was there little awareness of potential distractions, over-dependence on technology, or overconfidence?

Score: _____

Comment: _____

_____

3. How have you gone about ensuring accuracy and consistency in a document or data you were preparing? Tell me about a specific case in which your attention to detail paid off.

   Expected answer: Did the candidate take clear precautions such as proofing thoroughly, double-checking, verifying format consistency, etc.? Was there only a cursory spot check?

   Score: _____

   Comment: _____

   _____

4. Tell me about your experience in dealing with routine work. What kinds of problems did you have to overcome in order to concentrate on the details of the job?

   Expected answer: Did the candidate use a strategy to maintain attentiveness during routine work? Was there acceptance of diminished alertness, with little effort being made to remove/reduce it?

   Score: _____

   Comment: _____

   _____

5. Give me an example that demonstrates your ability to organize and maintain a system of records.

   Expected answer: Did the candidate initiate or show commitment to a systematic method for organization or record keeping? Was there ineffective record keeping, overconfidence in memory, or dependence on others?

   Score: _____

   Comment: _____

   _____

Initiative

Initiative includes the ability to bring about great results from ordinary circumstances, prepare for problems or opportunities in advance, transform leads into productive business outcomes, undertake additional responsibilities, and respond to situations as they arise without supervision.

1. Tell me about a situation in which you aggressively capitalized on an opportunity and converted something ordinary into something special

    Expected answer: Did the candidate put a unique twist on a routine situation to yield unusually positive results, probably not achieved by others in similar situations? Was there an accomplishment of little magnitude or that should have been expected of anyone in that situation?

    Score: _____

    Comment: _____
    _____

2. Describe something you've done that shows how you can respond to situations as they arise without supervision.

    Expected answer: Did the candidate take reasonable and quick action with an appropriate amount of information or research, warranting the independence? Was there use of authority inappropriately, excess procrastination, or a bad decision?

    Score: _____

    Comment: _____
    _____

3. Describe a time when you voluntarily undertook a special project above and beyond your normal responsibilities.

   Expected answer: Did the candidate volunteer for a large task/responsibility despite an already full workload and succeed without undue compromise of other responsibilities? Was there an insignificant, short-term addition, or an unnecessary sacrifice of other areas?

   Score: _____

   Comment: _____
   _____

4. Many people have good ideas, but few act on them. Tell me how you've transformed a good idea into a productive business outcome.

   Expected answer: Did the candidate generate a meaningful action plan to bring the idea to reality? Was there a haphazard, unrealistic, or unproductive transformation?

   Score: _____

   Comment: _____
   _____

Index

#

#define 233
#endif 234
#include 233
#pragma 233

<

\<blockquote\> 99

A

AACBS .See American Assembly of Collegiate Business Schools, See American Assembly of Collegiate Business Schools
ACID 211
  Atomicity *212*
  Consistency *212*
  Durability *213*
  Isolation *212*
Adobe Photoshop 107, 109
American Assembly of Collegiate Business Schools
.... 26, 28
Apache 175
Appearance 70
Application client container .. 209
Application tuning 44
Attrition 12, 50, 86, 93

B

Background check 24, 73
Behavior 69
Body language 69
Brain Bench 66
Business majors 28

C

CAPTCHA 105
Cartesian product 153
Cascading Style Sheets 103
CASE tools 15
Cisco IOS 179
colspan 101
Common job duties 42
  Determine user requirements *43*
  Liaison *43*
  Produce specifications *42*
  Provide technical expertise *43*
  Testing application functionality *43*
Communication skills 45
Computer scientists 28
Continuus 16, 189
Cost of hiring 50
CSS 102, 103, 104
CVS 16, 189

D

Demeanor 69
  Diction *69*
  Eye Contact *69*
  Fidgeting *69*
DMZ 181
Dreamweaver 137

E

EAR .... *See* Enterprise Archive

ebXML 15
Education majors 28
EIS ... *See* Enterprise Information System
EJB ...... *See* Enterprise JavaBeans
EJB container 200, 204, 209
Empathetic Employee 93
Engineers 27
Enterprise Archive 206
Enterprise Information System
 .... 208, 209
Enterprise Java Beans 227
Enterprise JavaBeans 204, 226
Enterprise Resource Planning
 208
entity bean 200
ERD diagrams 43
ERP .... *See* Enterprise Resource Planning
ERP Systems 17
EXPLAIN PLAN 154
explain_table 154

F

Flash 164
Flex time 11
Flextime 92
fraudulent applicant 29
Fraudulent Work History 23
FTP 117

G

Golden handcuffs 12
Gourman Report 27, 29
GROUP BY 152
Gung-Ho Employee 93

H

Hiring phases 59
Home Interface 201
HttpServlet 202
HttpServletRequest 202
HttpServletResponse 202

I

Idempotent Header Files 244
IIOP .... *See* Internet Inter-ORB Protocol
InitialContext 199
IntelliJ IDEA 189
Internet Inter-ORB Protocol 213
Internic 105
intrusion detection systems 185
IP address 106
IPv4 182
IT headhunters 52

J

JAR 206, 207, 213
Java Message Service 214
Java Remote Method Protocol
 205
Java Server Pages 216
Java Transaction API 214
Java Virtual Machine 214, 226
javac 192
JavaOne[SM] 12
JavaScript 121
JBuilder 189, 226
JDBC 76
JDeveloper 189, 226
JMS .... *See* Java Message Service
Job Titles 12

JRMP..... *See* ava Remote Method Protocol
JUnit.. 43
JVM...... *See* Java Virtual Machine

L

Language-Adaptable Header Files 244
loop structures 152

M

main()..................................... 192
malloc()................................... 242
Management by Objective 12
Math majors 28
MBA.. 14
mod_backhand 176
mod_bandwidth 176
mod_jk 177
mod_perl 177
mod_rewrite 176
mod_status 175
mod_throttle 176
Muic majors 28
MySQL 17, 140, 147, 176, 188
mysqlbinlog............................ 148

N

NAT........... *See* Network Address Translation
Network Address Translation 183

O

On-site interview 75
OPC ..... *See* Other People's Code

Opportunities for advancement 87
Oracle Call Interface 157
Oracle SCM 16
Oracle Software Configuration Management 189
ORDER BY 152
Other People's Code 31

P

packet sniffer 178
Perl 76, 169, 177, 201
Personal integrity 24
Personality................................ 32
    Curiosity 34
    Detail-oriented 38
    Polite manners 35
    Self-confidence 33
    Self-starting 36
    Tenacity 35
PHP 129, 140, 157
print().................................... 194
println() 194
printStackTrace() 194
public classes 190

R

Really Simple Syndication...... 102
References............................... 72
Remote Interface 201
Remote Method Invocation . 204, 214
résumé falsifications 29
Resume Red Flags.................... 60
Résumé screening 23, 62
reverse proxy 176

Index **287**

RMI .... *See* Remote Method Invocation
rowspan 102
RSS 102

S

Salaries 10, 91
SCCS ...... *See* UNIX Source Code Control System
Scientist Employee 93
Security 178
Session Bean 201
smurf attack 185
SOAP 15
SSL 105
STAR schema design 15
stateful 179
stateless 179
SYN flood 186
System.out.print() 194
System.out.println() 194

T

TCP/IP 106, 117, 182
Technical assessment 59
Technical examination 66
Telecommuting 12, 92
Telephone interview 59, 64, 66, 78
Telephone screening 64
Thawte Consulting 184
TKPROF 154

Troubleshooting 35, 43, 44, 53
Tuition reimbursement 89

U

UDDI 15
UML .... *See* Unified Modeling Language
UML diagrams 43
Unified Modeling Language .. 211
UNIX Source Code Control System 16
URL parameter 140
Use Cases 43
utlxplan.sql 154

V

Verisign 184
Virtual Private Network 181
Visual Age for Java 226
VPN *See* Virtual Private Network

W

W3C 104
WAR .... *See* Web archive
WDSL 15
Web archive 207
Web container 204, 210

X

XML 15, 102, 145, 199, 206

About Janet Burleson

As a top executive with BEI, Janet Burleson has extensive experience recruiting, hiring and managing Information Technology professionals.

As an expert Web design consultant Janet provides high level Web consulting services that improve the market status of Fortune 500 companies including Web search rank positioning, keyword optimization, Web content optimization, Web community relationships, Web site design, Web usage tracking and Web site configuration.

Janet is also one of the world's pioneering horse trainers, having developed the successful Guide Horse Foundation donating her time and effort to train miniature horses to guide the blind.
www.guidehorse.com

About Mike Reed

When he first started drawing, Mike Reed drew just to amuse himself. It wasn't long, though, before he knew he wanted to be an artist.

Today he does illustrations for children's books, for magazines, for catalogs, and for ads.

He also teaches illustration at the College of Visual Art in St. Paul, Minnesota. Mike Reed says, "Making pictures is like acting — you can paint yourself into the action." He often paints on the computer, but he also draws in pen and ink and paints in acrylics. He feels that learning to draw well is the key to being a successful artist.

Mike is regarded as one of the nation's premier illustrators and is the creator of the popular "Flame Warriors" illustrations at **www.flamewarriors.com**. A renowned children's artist, Mike has also provided the illustrations for dozens of children's books.

Mike Reed has always enjoyed reading. As a young child, he liked the Dr. Seuss books. Later, he started reading biographies and war stories. One reason why he feels lucky to be an illustrator is because he can listen to books on tape while he works. Mike is available to provide custom illustrations for all manner of publications at reasonable process. Mike can be reached at **www.mikereedillustration.com**.

Conducting the UNIX Job Interview

IT Manager Guide with UNIX Interview Questions

Adam Haeder

ISBN 0-9744355-6-2

Retail Price $16.95 / £10.95

This book is the accumulated observations of the authors' interviews with hundreds of job candidates. The author provides useful insights into what characteristics make a good UNIX programmer and offer their accumulated techniques as an aid to interviewing an UNIX job candidate.

This handy guide has a complete set of UNIX job interview questions and provides a complete method for accurately accessing the technical abilities of UNIX job candidates. By using UNIX job interview questions that only an experienced person knows, your supervisor can ask the right interview questions and fill your UNIX job with the best qualified UNIX developer.

Assists the IT manager in choosing the best-qualified UNIX professionals.

Provides proven techniques that can accurately ascertain a job candidate's suitability for an UNIX position.

www.Rampant-Books.com

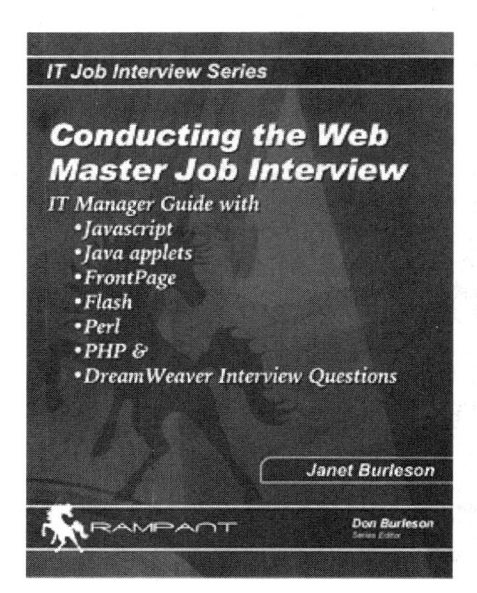

Conducting the Web Master Job Interview

IT Manager Guide with Interview Questions

Janet Burleson

ISBN 0-9745993-1-X

Retail Price $16.95 / £10.95

As a professional web master, Janet Burleson has extensive experience interviewing web master job candidates. With over a decade of interviewing experience, Burleson tell you how to quickly identify acceptable web master job candidates by asking the right web master job interview questions.

This book is the accumulated observations of the author's interviews with hundreds of job candidates. The author provides useful insights into what characteristics make a good web master programmer and offers her accumulated techniques as an aid to interviewing a web master job candidate.

This handy guide has a complete set of web master job interview questions and provides a complete method for accurately assessing the technical abilities of web master job candidates. By using web master job interview questions that only an experienced person knows, your supervisor can ask the right interview questions and fill your web master job with the best qualified web master developer.

www.Rampant-Books.com

Conducting the J2EE Job Interview

IT Manager Guide for J2EE with Interview Questions

Jeffrey M. Hunter

ISBN 0-9744355-9-7

Retail Price $16.95 / £10.95

This book is the accumulated observations of the author's interviews with hundreds of job candidates. The author provides useful insights into what characteristics make a good J2EE programmer and offers his accumulated techniques as an aid to interviewing a J2EE programmer job candidate.

This handy guide has a complete set of J2EE job interview questions and provides a complete method for accurately assessing the technical abilities of J2EE job candidates. By using J2EE job interview questions that only an experienced person knows, your application developers can ask the right interview questions and fill your J2EE job with the best qualified J2EE developer.

www.Rampant-Books.com

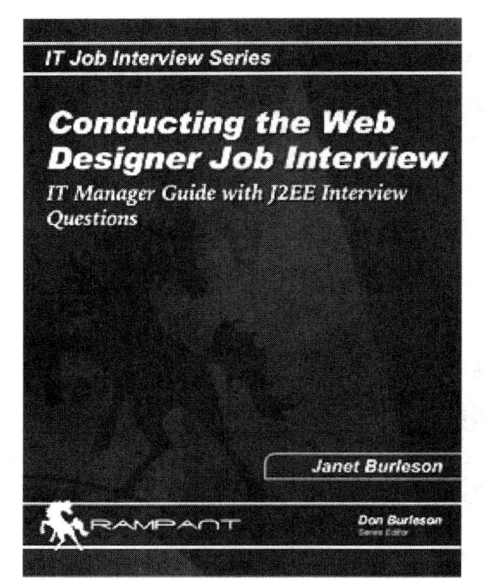

Conducting the Computer Programmer Job Interview

IT Manager Guide with C, C++, Cobol, UNIX shell & Oracle Interview Questions

Janet Burleson

ISBN 0-9745993-2-8

Retail Price $16.95 / £10.95

This book is the accumulated observations of the authors' programmer job interviews with hundreds of job candidates. The author provides useful insights into what characteristics make a good computer programmer, and offer their accumulated techniques as an aid to interviewing a programmer job candidate.

This handy guide has a complete set of programmer job interview questions and provides a complete method for accurately accessing the technical abilities of programmer job candidates. By using computer programmer job interview questions that only an experienced programmer knows, you can ask the right interview questions and fill your programmer job with the best qualified programmer.

www.Rampant-Books.com

Conducting the Oracle Job Interview

IT Manager's Guide for Oracle Job Interviews with Oracle Interview Questions

Mike Ault & Don Burleson

ISBN 0-9727513-1-9
Publication Date – February, 2003

Retail Price $16.95 / £10.95

As professional consultants, Don Burleson and Mike Ault have interviewed hundreds of Oracle job candidates. With over four decades of interviewing experience, Ault and Burleson tell you how to quickly identify acceptable Oracle job candidates by asking the right Oracle job interview questions.

Mike Ault and Don Burleson are recognized as the two best-selling Oracle Authors in the world. With combined authorship of over 25 books, Ault & Burleson are the two most respected Oracle authorities on the planet. For the first time ever, Ault & Burleson combine their talents in this exceptional handbook.

Using Oracle job interview questions that are not available to the general public, the IT manager will be able to quickly access the technical ability of any Oracle job candidate. In today's market, there are thousands of under-trained Oracle professionals, and the IT manager must be able to quickly access the true ability of the Oracle job candidate.

www.Rampant-Books.com

Free!
Oracle 10g Senior DBA Reference Poster

This 24 x 36 inch quick reference includes the important data columns and relationships between the DBA views, allowing you to quickly write complex data dictionary queries.

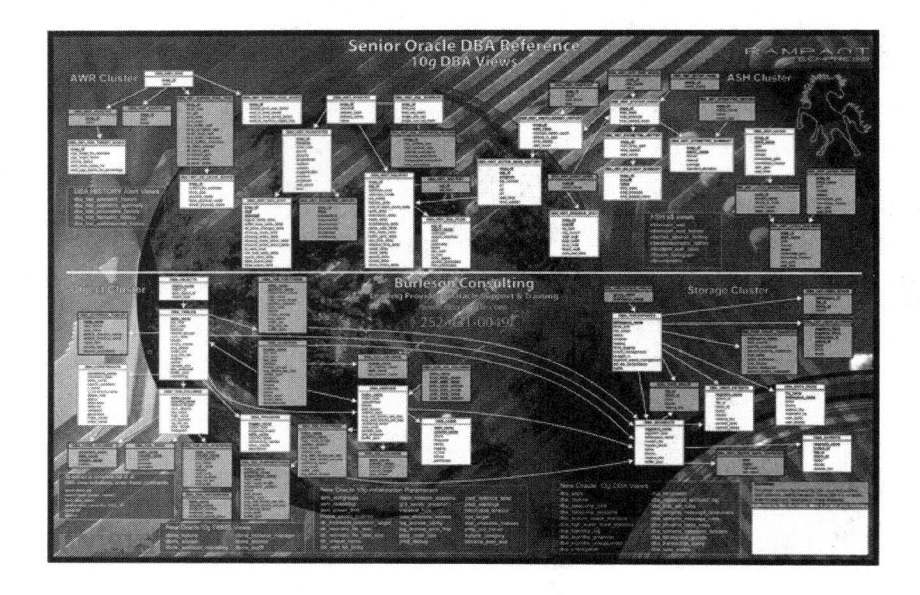

This comprehensive data dictionary reference contains the most important columns from the most important Oracle10g DBA views. Especially useful are the Automated Workload Repository (AWR) and Active Session History (ASH) DBA views.

WARNING - This poster is not suitable for beginners. It is designed for senior Oracle DBAs and requires knowledge of Oracle data dictionary internal structures. You can get your poster at this URL:

> www.rampant.cc/poster.htm